AFRICAN MUSLIM NAMES:
IMAGES AND IDENTITIES

AFRICAN MUSLIM NAMES: IMAGES AND IDENTITIES

SHARIFA M. ZAWAWI

Africa World Press, Inc.

P.O. Box 1892

Trenton, NJ 08607

P.O. Box 48

Asmara, ERITREA

Africa World Press, Inc.

P.O. Box 1892	P.O. Box 48
Trenton, NJ 08607	Asmara, ERITREA

Copyright © 1998 Sharifa M. Zawawi

First Printing 1998

Cover and Book : Jonathan Gullery

This book is set in Palatino

Library of Congress Cataloging-in-Publication Data

Zawawi, Sharifa
    African Muslim names: images and identities / by Sharifa M.
Zawawi.
       p. cm.
       ISBN 0-86543-572-3. -- ISBN 0-86543-573-1 (pbk.)
       1. Names, Personal--African. 2. Names, personal--Muslim.
I. Title.
    CS2375.A33Z39 1998
    929.4'096--dc21   98-22129
                                           CIP

Allaahu laa ilaaha illaa huwa.
lahuu-l-asmaau-l-Husnaa.
God, there is no deity except Him.
His are the most beautiful names.[1]

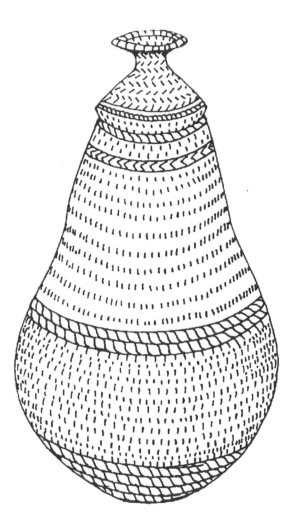

CONTENTS

INTRODUCTION

THE CHILDREN

Those many children running in your space
Have you named them
or shall the gardens do it?
Those green children
climb from the pit
or do they descend
from the mountain top?

These very tiny children
I see now like fish
of many colors
in the fishbowl of space.
You are their water.[2]

The matter of names raises perennial questions. This book begins with the title of my previous one, *What's in a Name: Unaitwaje?*, but this time the subject matter is more specific: *What's in an African Muslim name?* The present book answers this new question. *African Muslim Names: Images and Identities*, provides an overview of African Muslim names, illustrates their adaptation to African languages, and reveals the synthesis that comes about between the indigenous and the Islamic. Above all, this book discusses the meanings of African Muslim names and relates them to the contexts in which they appear.

A 'name' is simply a word, phrase or sentence by which a human being is known. By it, s/he is identified, called, described, distinguished and classified. Nothing on this earth—and in much of the heavens—exists without a name. There are names for people, things, buildings and places, and also for storms and hurricanes. Man-made and natural phenomena alike are known through their names.

What's in a name? A name conveys history, culture, heritage, language and a consciousness of self-image and pride. An Islamic name may in certain contexts also signify an ideological, social and political stand. In short, our names convey our existences and our images of ourselves.[3] Onomastics or the study of names invites many disciplines: history, geography, linguistics, literature, philosophy, anthropology, psychology, sociology, theology, even legal studies. It engages concern with character, personality, adoption, education, marriage, conversion, migration and death. In all, identity is the underlying feature and the principal one.

Personal names provide an important component of African cultural identities.[4] They reach across ethnic, geographical and national boundaries and extend identity from the African continent to the Pan-African diaspora. Names, like language itself, provide their bearers with a sense of oneness in spite of ethnic differences. They bestow social and economic openness and invite participation. The first thing an African wants to know when he or she meets you is your name.

A name is all too often taken for granted. For an African, names and naming operate significantly to maintain social links and in the development of a culture and an individual. To quote an Ilaje proverb:

Oruko mi ro nen, apeja mi ro nen
As the name, so is the bearer,
like the nickname, like the bearer's.[5]

Or, as the Waswahili say:

Wewe na jina lako.
You and your name.
You are what your name has made you.

Names symbolize social organization. They indicate ethnic and tribal affiliation, status, privilege, gender, religion and achievement within specific contexts. They transmit historical and cultural information. A name is essential in establishing connections with one's kin and with one's community and in weighing the essence of a person or thing. The one who names an object, a place or a person often has control over the relevance of that person, place or thing. Adam was taught all the names so that he might have knowledge and power to use them. Every human being, male and female, is his own Adam entrusted in his knowledge and commanded with a responsibility for the good of humanity and for all contemporary and future generations.[6]

African Muslim names present a common cultural heritage extending from west to east and north to south crossing national and racial borders and at times even religious boundaries. First and foremost these names are based on the concept of a human being in relation to the Creator of all, whether he is referred to by the Arabic name of Allah and his numerous attributes, or by his Swahili equivalent, Mwenye-Enzi-Mngu (the Almighty), Mola (Master), or Rabi (My Guardian) or by the Hausa-Fulani name of Maa Ngala (Master of All), Masa Dembali (Infinite Master) or Dundari (the Supreme One). This concept is the foundation of the way of life and nomenclature of all African Muslims.

The coexistence of Islamic and traditional African beliefs has resulted in an African-Islamic culture that is prevalent not only among the Hausa-Fulani and Waswahili on the continent, but also beyond the continent in the diaspora. In the course of acquiring Islamic-Arabic culture and becoming integrated into the worldwide Muslim community, Africans adopted Islamic Arabic names. The young are instructed in the religion by teaching them a moral way of life. This teaching and the knowledge derived from it arous-

xiii

es in them a consciousness of their relationship with their Creator and with the universe. Traditional folk stories and proverbs continue the task that names begin.

African names used by Muslims and non-Muslims also show how people identify with their culture and heritage. In addition a name identifies the family's desired image or personality for their child and is considered a dominant aspect in the development of his character and personality. A good name gives a good feeling, a bad name gives a bad feeling about oneself. A child who is called a king, Maalik/Maliik, or a Kariim, a generous one, may feel like one.

Newborns are named for many different reasons: they inherit a name of a relative to maintain family links; they capture or symbolize an idea to communicate a message or record an event; they may carry names to remind them of the qualities inspired by those who have chosen them. These qualities often draw on spiritual and human values: compassion (RaHiim and Rehema), justice ('Adil and 'Adila), generosity (Kariim and Kariima), gratefulness (AbdulHamiid and Hamiida), wisdom ('Aqiil and 'Aqiila), faithfulness (Amiin and Amiina), truthfulness (Sadiiq and Sadiqa), patience (Sabuur and Sabbuura), bravery (Abduljabbar and Jasira) and love (Habiib and Habiiba). All these masculine and feminine names have meanings, purpose and significance. They designate, describe and identify the individual. They contribute towards self-esteem and a concern for others. They often precede the bearer and outlast him. They are connected to a desired image. In the process of naming, people preserve and mould their moral values and their social history.

Names are therefore words with meanings possessing historical context. Thus the name MusTafa has a historical context of relating it to the character of a prophet. At the same time, for those who know the Arabic language, it has semantic significance. It signifies a special person, the chosen one. Similarly, the girl's name FaaTma is popular not simply because of its meaning as one who is knowledgeable and is outstanding, but even more because of its link to Prophet MuHammad. FaaTma was the name of one of his four daughters. She was the wife of his cousin Ali bin Abi Talib and the mother of his grandsons, Hassan and Hussein.

Names of this type and some biblical names, such as Nuhu, Musa, Yakubu, Yahya, Yusufu, Yunusa and Haruna, are used in Africa not only by Muslims but by Christians as well. They may appear in these Islamic forms, as well as in the Christian names Noah, Moses, Jacob, John, Joseph, Jenus and Aaron. One encounters names such as Rev. Victor Musa, Rev. Bako Yusufu, Karolyn Ali, Sheikh Shaaban bin Robert, Hakeem Olajuwon, Malik Yoba, Muhammad Askia, Muhammad Marmaduke. These names of certain and not so familiar intermix are familiar combinations in Africa and the world. This is part of our interdependent world of intercultural exchange and an important aspect of ancient and modern African customs and traditions.

Yet, surprisingly, very little attention has been paid to the cultural distinctiveness and social importance of names for African and Pan-African culture. Although much has been written about African culture and its relation to other global cultures, the communicative aspect of names and naming among Africans has not received much attention.[7] Muslim names in Africa have received even less attention, and there has been no study whatever of the form, purpose, content and significance of Muslim names among Africans of the diaspora.[8]

Names are among the most important ways in which believers preserve their Muslim identity and maintain their spiritual, moral and social values. Because of this, revealing the meanings and significance of the African Muslim names is important if we are to understand the religious, social and cultural aspects of a life shared by inhabitants of a large part of Africa. At the same time it is interesting to notice the differences, modifications and linguistic changes that occur across the cultural groups of East and West Africa represented in these names. They reveal past histories and events, some of which they have in common, in some of which they differ.

A name reflects and reinforces an identity both when it is given and when it is changed. An interest in African cultural identity has been the subject of numerous publications, but very little attention has been given to the use of Muslim names among Africans of the continent or in the diaspora.[9]

African Muslim Names: Images and Identities fills this gap. The names that appear have necessarily to be a small selection from among the many that exist because this is a short book. The names introduced here come mainly from two languages - Hausa-Fulani and Kiswahili. These are the two major African languages which are spoken as lingua franca by millions of people throughout the African continent.[10]

This book will be of special interest to parents and relatives searching for names for their newborn. In these days of mounting interest in identity and culture, this book will serve the needs of many Muslim Africans, African-Americans and others who may wish to know the meanings of the names they choose. From it they will learn their social and cultural significance. They will be able to select names not only on the basis of their sound, but as reflecting their aspirations for their children and themselves. For non-Muslims the book will contribute cultural knowledge to today's discourse on the values and aspirations of people of different faiths. Given the long history of Islam in Africa, Muslim names communicate an old civilization encompassing a multicultural community. The book will also be useful to anyone interested in African languages and language contact throughout the continent. The world is not only united and divided by its languages and their vocabularies. It is united and divided by names.

Before discussing African Muslim names, a general discussion of the continent and its complexity is imperative. Africa, a vast continent three times the size of Europe and four times of the United States, has according to some estimates fifty-four states and a diverse population speaking as many as a thousand related languages. It is also a continent of many cultural forms of names and naming significant for ethnic group and individual identity and identification.

This study draws on two main sources. First it examines Muslim names and naming in the Qur'aan, the Muslim holy scripture, and in the Sunna, stories or traditions about the Prophet MuHammad. Secondly, it draws heavily on African literature and journalism, lists compiled for me by friends from West and East Africa, contacts I have made with students over the past three decades and telephone directories from Nigeria, Kenya and Tanzania.

The book contains seven chapters, notes and a list of abbreviations and of references. Lists of masculine and feminine names, arranged in alphabetical order, appear in Part Two. I discuss variant spellings and usages and provide help in pronunciation. The status of names as features of identification, social control and training, as well as ways of relating to one's ancestors or maintaining one's heritage, is discussed. This book establishes the thesis that African Muslim names are derived from words that have their context in a language and time, are meaningful and are chosen with great care and affection.

NOTES

1. The Qur'aan, Surat T a-ha, 20, verse 8.
2. Qasim Haddad (born 1948 in Bahrain),translated by Sharif Elmusa and Charles Doria in Salma Khadra Jayyusi, *Modern Arabic Poetry*, p. 232.
3. Scholarly discussions on names and naming by social scientists are numerous. Several journals on the subject exist, among them the famous or not so famous journal on Names, *Journal of the American Name Society*.
4. As I have indicated in my previous book, besides having a psychological role in establishing a person's identity, names convey, to those who know their origin and meaning, the social and cultural experiences of the people who have created them. They

also reveal historical and political contacts between people. Above all, names depict how members of a community regard themselves (1993:1).

5. Ojoade, p.196.

6. See below for the meaning and significance of the name Adam.

7. Asante notes: Since behavior and attitude are tied directly to a person's sense of self esteem and importance, the choice of name should not be left to chance or simply drawn from a lottery, it should be well thought out, discussed, and then decided upon (1991:11). Mazrui is in favor of the use of indigenous names and suggests three major innovations: Pan-Africanization of African names, the ecumenicalization and the androgynization of African names. *The Africans: A Triple Heritage*,1986: 253-7.

8. The importance of African names is recognized in Nia Damali's *Golden Names for an African People: African & Arabic Names* (1986). 'Everywhere in Africa, the name is considered a distinct part of the individual. There is something like a material and physical affinity between a man and his name; a person can be hurt through his name, and to avoid this it is sometimes kept secret. To pronounce the name is to act on the soul,to provoke it, is to constrain it (Erny 1973:142), (Damali 1986: Foreword).
Books have been written about Arabic, Indian, Pakistani, Persian and Turkish Muslim names, yet, remarkably, these books totally ignore Africa an extensive region of the globe where Islamic cultural influence is also prevalent and extensive.

9. Among the latest works on African identity is Mazrui and Shariff's, *The Swahili: Idiom and Identity of an African People*, Lawrenceville, NJ: Africa World Press, Inc. 1993, and Middleton, John, *The World of the Swahili*, New Haven and London, Yale University Press, 1992.

10. The 1966 *World Almanac* gives 38 million Hausa speakers in Northern Nigeria, Niger and Cameroon and 49 million Swahili speakers in Kenya, Tanzania, Zaire and Uganda. There are more speakers of these two languages in the other African states.

CHAPTER ONE

WHAT'S IN A MUSLIM NAME?

The Islamic world stretches across all continents. Islam as a world religion spread in the seventh century from Mecca and Medina in Arabia, to Asia, Africa and beyond. It has not only been adopted by millions of people of different races, color and nationality, but it has influenced many of those with whom Muslims came into contact and who now share its culture. The name Islam means to submit one's self to worshipping the One and only God who created human beings and everything above, below and around them.[1] The root s-l-m means peace and the verb salima means to be safe from harm. Islam means to be at peace with God, with one's self and with one's fellow beings:

> wa jaahidu fii-llaahi Haqqa jihaadihi huwa jtabaakum
> wa maa ja'ala 'alaykum fii-d-diin min Haraji millata
> abiikum ibraahiima huwa samaakum-l-muslimiina
> min qablu wa fii hadhaa liyakuuna r-rasuulu shahi-
> idan 'alaykum wa takuunu shuhadaa'a 'alaa-n-naasi
> fa aqiimu-S-Salaata wa atuuu-z-akaata wa 'taSimuu
> bi-llaahi huwa mawlaakum fani'ma l-mawlaa wa
> ni'ma n-naSiir.

And strive for God's sake, the way He should be striven for. He has chosen you and has not laid upon you in faith any hardship; the sect of your forefather Ibrahiim. He has named you Muslims both previously and right now, so that the messenger may be a witness for you, and that you may be witness for mankind. So establish worship, pay alms, and hold fast to God; He is your Protector and your splendid Supporter.

Islam is a code of conduct and a way of life for all. Technically and linguistically, a child is born a Muslim and may be identified by a Muslim name. As an adult, a Muslim is anyone who submits to the worship of God and believes:

Laa Ilaaha Illaa-llaah, MuHammadu Rasuulu-llaah.

There is no God but the One God and MuHammad is His Prophet.

This unity or oneness of God is known as *tawHiid*, and a Muslim's consciousness of one's relationship to God is of utmost spiritual and ritual importance.[2] *TawHiid* has great significance for names and naming. As a religious practice, Islam does not belong to any special or chosen people and does not allow distinctions or discriminations of color, race or nation. It does not encourage extremism of any sort. Man and woman have the same origin and possess equal capabilities for intellectual, spiritual and moral attainment.[3] The Qur'aan is crystal clear on the dignity and equality of mankind, and it is the same today as it was in the days of Prophet MuHammad.

yaa ayyuhaa nnaasu innaa khalaqnaakum min dhakarin wa unthaa wa ja'alnaakum shu'uuban wa qabaaila lita'aarafuu inna akramakum 'inda llaahi atqaakum inna llaha 'aliimun khabiir.

O mankind! Lo! We have created you male and female, and have made you nations and tribes that you may know one another. Lo! the noblest among you, in the sight of God, is the best in conduct. Lo! God is all-knowing, aware.[4]

According to this verse the only judge of who is the best person is the Creator, the Almighty, the One who is to be worshipped and to be represented. Adam the first human being and ibn Adam, 'the son of Adam', the human being, is a *Khalifa*, a successor, a vicegerent of Allah, the One whom s/he represents. Thus a human being is endowed with a conscience, responsibility and accountability to his fellow man, and is himself entitled to freedom, respect and justice.

Muslims get their knowledge of religion from the Qur'aan which was revealed to MuHammad, its Prophet, the last of a line of many other prophets including Abraham, Moses and Jesus. MuHammad was born in Mecca in A.D. 570, fifty-four years before Hijra (his emigration to Medina). He died in A.D. 632 in Medina. Both his parents died before he was seven years old and he spent the early part of his life as a trader. As a Prophet he focused on the importance of character, education and work,[5] on the evils of corruption and on freedom of worship. Quoting the Qur'aan:

There is no compulsion in the matter of faith.[6]

The Muslim scripture was revealed to Prophet MuHammad in the Arabic language and it is this that has been preserved in the Qur'aan. Muslims believe that the Qur'aan is the Word of God as were other scriptures that appeared before it. It is said that the Qur'aan was memorized by many people during the Prophet's lifetime and was then collected and edited by him and by his widow Hafsa bint 'Umar. Their copy was left with Abuu Bakar, who became the first khalifa after the death of the Prophet in A.D.632. Many translations and commentaries of the Qur'aan have since been published in various languages but the original Arabic version is still the pre-eminent text. It is used by Muslims not only for recitation but as a literary source *par excellence*. It is the fountainhead of their verbal and written expression and a source of their values.

AFRICA AND ISLAM

Islam spread beyond the bounds of Arabia to Africa. It was introduced to the Ethiopian (Abyssinian) King (Negus) by Prophet MuHammad who sent a letter to the Christian king in A.D. 615. The Prophet also encouraged those of his followers who were persecuted in Mecca by the Quraish, his relatives, to migrate to Abyssinia. The first Muslim officer to reach Africa was 'Amr ibn Al-'aaS who arrived in Egypt around A.D. 639. He was followed by 'Uqba ibn Naafil who conquered Ifriiqiya (the Maghrib) and established a camp at Qayrawaan (Cairo) in A.D.670. Later Islam was carried throughout much of Africa by religious scholars, ('ulamaa'), by sufi teachers and their followers, and by traders. Abdul-Rahman Ibrahim Doi, a Nigerian author,[7] has demonstrated that Islam and West Africa have been closely connected since the dawn of Al-Islam. By the year A.D.850 the Dya'ogo dynasty in the kingdom of Tekrur had accepted Islam. The empires of Kanem-Borun, Songhay, Mali and the Hausa states accepted Islam between the eleventh and fourteenth centuries. Today, two-thirds of the total Muslim population south of the Sahara—some seventeen million people—live in West Africa.

Most are to be found in Nigeria, Senegal, Guinea, Mali, Gambia and Niger but smaller Muslim communities of minority traders and settlers are also found in Liberia, Ghana and Togo.[8]

Muslims moved to East Africa in large numbers at the time of 'Abdul-Malik bin Marwaan (A.D.683-5) during the period of the Umayyad dynasty which ruled from Damascus. Later people of Shiraaz in Persia traded and settled on its coasts. Kilwa, Sofala, Zanzibar, Pemba and Dar es-Salaam on the Tanzania coast, and Pate, Lamu and Mombasa on the Kenya coast, became important centers of trade and of Islamic settlement and religion. The Swahili traders of this Zinj Empire established its capital first at Kilwa and from there extended their trade to Sofala, Mozambique, Tabora, Ujiji and Zaire. By the ninth century Islam had reached as far south as Sofala, as observed and recorded by Abu-l-Hasan

4

'Ali Al-Mas'uudii, a historian from Baghdad in Iraq, in his *Muruuj al-dhahab wa Ma'aadinu-l-jawhar (The Meadows of Gold and the Gem Mines)*. Al-Mas'uudii died in A.D.956. Later Muslim contacts reached as far south as Zimbabwe, Madagascar and South Africa. Muslims are to be found on the coasts of Kenya and Tanzania and the islands of Pemba and Zanzibar. Today about a third of the total population of Ethiopia, Eritrea and Tanzania are Muslims and there are Muslim communities in Kenya, Uganda, Malawi, Sudan, Somalia, Zambia and Zaire.[9] Wherever Muslims went the Arabic language and script went with them.

The Arabic language and script preceded the religion. Africans first encountered Arabic through their contact with Arab traders, immigrants and travellers who had travelled from Yaman and Oman and reached Africa long before the coming of Islam. Long before the First Egyptian dynasty, East Africans sailed the Azania ocean; inscriptions on the walls of the tombs of Karnak show that Arab traders travelled to Punt on the eastern coast of Africa as early as 2000 B.C.[10] Trade between Africa and Asia is also recorded as early as the first century A.D. in *The Periplus of the Erythrean Sea*.

The Arabic language and its script, in conjunction with local languages, played a pre-eminent role in providing the linguistic expression of Islam, trade and culture. In Timbuktu, Sankore was both a rich trade center and a center of scholarship and learning where Arabic and Qur'anic doctrine and literature were taught and studied as early as the fourteenth century. Today Arabic is the mother tongue of over 190 million people world wide and the religious language for over 250 million. Arabic words are to be found in the vocabularies of many African languages east and west from Ge'ez, Amharic, Argobba, Gurage, Harari, Tigre, and Tigrinya in Ethiopia and Fulfulde (Fulani), Kanuri, Mandingo, Hausa, Yoruba in Nigeria and Wolof in Senegal.[11] Today two vast African contact languages, Hausa and Kiswahili, carry Islamic culture to non-Islamic regions throughout the continent.

Wherever Muslims live in Africa their communities are multireligious, multicultural and multilingual. Influences from other African religions, Judaism and Christianity contribute to their complexity. Yet they share elements of Universal Islam, specific Islamic traditions and a common value system.

They also have in common certain pan-Islamic cultural features. The Qur'aan and the Sunna (traditions of Prophet MuHammad) are the source and content of the faith and way of life of Muslim Africans. Their Islamic institutions are derived from the teachings of the Qur'aan and are known as The Five Principles or Pillars. The Five Pillars of Islam are:

1) Shahaada, testifying that God is one and
   that MuHammad is his prophet,

2) Zakaat, alms giving,

3) Salaa, prayers,

4) Sawm, fasting the month of RamaDaan,

5) Hajj, pilgrimage to Mecca once in one's lifetime for those who have the means to fulfill this obligation. They observe the shari'a (Islamic law) and the Islamic calendar, and share some social customs and rituals connected with marriage, birth and death, superstitions and food taboos. These constitute Islam's mosaic.

In the course of acquiring Islamic-Arabic culture and becoming integrated into the worldwide Muslim community, Africans adopted Islamic Arabic names. The next chapter explores the historical background, source, form and content of these African Muslim names.

SWAHILI SOCIETY BEYOND THE COAST OF EAST AFRICA

The language that we now know as Kiswahili might be the same language that Al-JaHiZ referred to as Zinjji. This use of the term to refer to an African language spoken on the East African coast I discuss in my unpublished manuscript *Kiswahili Contact and Change: A Sociolinguistic Study of the East*

African Coast. In short, from Al-JaHiZ'account it appears that the language was used as a lingua franca by the inhabitants of the islands, the coast and the traders with whom they came in contact. This was confirmed by Al-Mas'udi in A.D. 916/917 who reported that the Muslims of Qanbaluu (Pemba) spoke Zinjiyya. African peoples were to be found living in the Arabian cities and towns. Al-JaHiz himself was an Arab of African descent living in Basra in Iraq.

Islam is the religion of more than 97% of the population of Zanzibar and Pemba and is at least one-third of Tanzania of which Zanzibar is now a part. Kiswahili is spoken today by a very large number of people living on these islands and on the East African mainland. In 1971, Swahili speakers were estimated to be forty five million people living in the eastern and central parts of Africa.[12] With the rapid spread of the language, thirty years later they must now be many more. Kiswahili is the first language for many of those who live in the coastal region, the saaHil or the Azaniya coast of East Africa. This region consists of Zanzibar and Pemba, other small islands off the coast and the Kenya and Tanzania coasts. Waswahili were originally people who had an Islamic culture derived from one or more of several different Islamic groups: from Oman, Yemen, Persia, India and Africa. People from all these places were influenced by the process of Islamization and as a result their language was influenced. They were heterogeneous in their ethnic composition but homogeneous in their religious culture and language. All Waswahili identify themselves by descent in their fathers' line and names.

The Swahili society and their language, literature and culture spread beyond the coast of East Africa, their original home, to the hinterland, to the Arabian Gulf states and beyond.

This African language shared linguistic and cultural elements with Hausa-Fulani because of their African origin and their close and lengthy contact with Islam and with the Arabic language.

HAUSA-FULANI SOCIETY BEYOND NIGERIA

The Hausa-Fulani society is found in the northern region of Nigeria, a large West African country which consists of thirty states with a population of over 110 million. According to the 1963 census 47.2 % of the total population are Muslims. Like the Waswahili in East Africa, there have been many speculations, myths and hypotheses about their origins resulting in many scholarly papers and publications.[13]The region is also rich in its local oral traditions of legends, folk tales and poetry that depict their ancestry and origin. The dispute lingers on their origin, their historical contacts, their ethnic and social identity, their relationship to Islam, and the nature of their languages.

People of many ethnicities live in Nigeria but the main groups are the Hausa-Fulani in the north, the Yoruba in the west and the Igbo (originally spelt Heeboo) in the east. The Hausa and the Fulani (the Fulbe or Fulfulde) are grouped together because of their history: they are mostly Muslims, have the same socio-cultural institutions and speak the Hausa language. Although the Hausa live mainly in the Sokoto, Kano and Kaduna States, their language is widely used by other Nigerians who live in other parts of the country and has shaped their culture.

To most Hausa people, language is one of the factors which persuade them to regard a stranger as Hausa: the person should be fluent in the Hausa language and in all his dealings with Hausa people he should use it as his first language. Though not all Hausa of the homeland were Muslims, Islam has for quite some time been a very powerful social landmark in the acculturating frontier of the Hausa as an ethnic group both at home and in migration, observes Mahdi Adamu.[14]

He goes on to define the Hausa as:

Those who historically issued from Hausaland or their descendants through the male line, or those who

8

became closely associated with Hausa culture by adopting its language, its customs and religion.[15]

In this definition Adamu includes the Fulanis.

Hausa, a language of the Chadic family, a subbranch of the Afro-Asiatic group of languages, is a lingua franca. Like Kiswahili it is a first language of many people who live in the northern states of Nigeria and the Niger Republic. It is also a language of interethnic communication spoken by millions of other West Africans. Because of long Hausa contact with Arabic and an affinity to Islam, it shares linguistic and cultural elements with Kiswahili. The contact of Hausa-speaking people with the Arabs and with the Arabic-speaking North Africans before 1000 A.D. developed as a result of the trans-Saharan trade, while that of Swahili East Africans and the Arabs came about through the southern (Indian) ocean trade. In both regions, with commerce came a mixture of people, language, script, religion, education, law, customs and traditions. As a result the Arabic language and script and Islamic value system have contributed immensely to Hausa-Fulani and Kiswahili. Both languages were written down in the Arabic form of script called Ajami in West Africa and Khati za Kiarabu on the Swahili coast. The two languages are now dominant major African languages south of the Sahara. Both have produced extensive and unique oral and written African literatures.

Although in Nigeria English is the official language of government and a pidgin English is also widely used, the major African languages such as Hausa, Yoruba, Igbo, Edu, Tiv, Fulfulde, Efik and others provide critical everyday connection. Important aspects of communication and socializing the young in maintaining the culture are done through native languages yet many of the songs, proverbs, folktales, riddles, games, superstitions and divinity have been expressed and recorded in Hausa in Nigeria and in Kiswahili in East Africa. All these forms of local enculturation serve to entertain, stimulate and to educate the African child. Although this traditional form of early education is now somewhat dying or

9

being neglected the names are still given and serve as an important part of socializing the child.

NOTES

1. This Oneness and Unity of God is clearly expressed in the Qur'aan, Al-IkhlaaS, Sura 112, Verses 1-4.
2. Qur'aan, Surat-ul-Hajj, 22 verse 78.
3. Gender discrimination is, wrongly, believed to characterize Islam.
4. Ibid. Sura 49, verse 13.
5. Among Prophet MuHammad's well-known sayings are: 'Seek knowledge even if you have to go to China' and 'Seeking knowledge is an obligation for every Muslim man and woman.'
6. Ibid. Suratu-l-Baqra, 2 verse 257.
7. See Doi's article on 'Islamic Thought and Culture: Their Impact on Africa and with Special Reference to Nigeria,' in *The Islamic Review and Arab Affairs* v. 57 Oct. 1969 pp. 18-23
8. Ibid pp.4-5.
9. Ibid p.5.
10. See Zawawi, 1993, p. 23.
11. The relationship of Yoruba to Arabic is discussed by Modupe Oduyoye, 'Yoruba and Semitic Languages: Linguistic Relationship' in the *Nigeria Magazine*, No.99, Dec. 1968 and in his *Yoruba Names: Their Structure & Meaning*, 1982. The connection of Yoruba with ancient Egyptian is discussed by Cheikh Anta Diop. See below, endnote on chapter Seven.
12. See Zawawi, 1971: 1.
13. The Hausas' as well as the Yorubas' oral traditions and legends trace their peoples' ancestors to migration from the Near East. This contact with the north is considered by historians a major factor of the development of the Kanem-Borno empire around Lake Chad and to its west the independent towns constituting the Hausa states. The famous African scholar, Cheikh Anta Diop, confirms their connection with ancient Egypt.
14. See his *The Hausa Factor in West African History*, Oxford University Press, 1978, p.4
15. Ibid. p.4

CHAPTER TWO

NAMES AND NAMING

HOW NAMES ARE CHOSEN

In African families children's names are chosen with much deliberation. A name and naming hold an important place in one's daily life. A name is like a seed that governs growth or a process which may turn out to be good or bad depending on the kind of seed from which the plant has sprouted. On a social level, a name contributes towards an individual's training and discipline. In these days of negative attitudes and psychological insecurity, good names should be used frequently as reminders of ethical behavior. They also function as means of identity and may determine one's feelings and attitudes towards oneself and others.

The first-born girl in an extended family is often named after a grandmother, a boy after a grandfather. A girl known as *Asha Masoud Salim* carries a female personal name of her grandmother but the rest of the names are of her father and grandfather. The boy *Salim Masoud Salim is a* grandchild who carries his grandfather's name: the name is passed down, as we say. Other children are given the names of other relatives such as aunts and uncles. Whenever there is a death within the kin group the name of the deceased person is likely to be inherited by the next newborn child. This means that there may be, for example, several boys named *Qais* in the same kin group, all born in the same year or shortly after one another. People believe that a child acquires not only the name but the qualities of his or her namesake.

A name may be chosen from the Qur'aan or a name book[1] or adopted at the suggestion of a relative, a religious leader, or a friend. It may be chosen to depict the circumstances of a child's birth.e.g. *Tabu or Mwatabu* a child of difficulty. Some names may indicate the actual moment, the day or time that a child is born, e.g.

SabiH/Sabiha	morning, beauty
Laila or	night
Chausiku	night

Or it may speak of a cheerful event that took place when the child was born e.g.

Suda	luck
Furaha	happiness
Safari	journey
Bahati	luck, prosperity in the family

The name may allude to something that was happening at the time the child came into the world, e.g.

Masika	heavy rainy season
Arusi	wedding
Hasaduna	they envied us

or it may describe the baby's appearance at birth

Jamaal; Jamila	handsome; beautiful
Kifimbo	thin
Samina, Manono	fat
Samra or Cheusi	dark-skinned
Reem	fair
Kilizi or Mkali	cry baby, quiet
Afya	healthy

The name given to a child may also reveal the parents' philosophy or hopes, e.g.

Maskini	poor, humble
Amal; Tumaini	hope

Parents sometimes choose two or three names and then consult an astrologer as to which is best for their child.[2]

RITUALS CONNECTED WITH NAMING

Rituals associated with a name and naming are religious and cultural but vary from society to society. Imagine you are born a Swahili Muslim child. Immediately after your birth and before having been shown the sun, you are informed of your Creator's greatness. Your father, a kinsman or a close friend whispers into your ear, *Allahu Akbar*, God is great. In the next breath you are told your name even if it is a temporary name. (A person must be given a name even if that person is unlikely to live long).

On your day of birth you may be given a taste of aloe and honey on your tongue, a symbol that life is both sweet and bitter. Your palate may be rubbed with a piece of softened date (known in Arabic as *taHniiq*) to accustom you to eating. This is a common Islamic tradition everywhere. Your mother will breastfeed you for the first two years but not a day more. During the two years, if she cannot produce the milk, another woman, your mother's relative or friend, will breastfeed you instead. Her children then become your siblings, through your sharing their mother's milk with them.

After your birth, you are introduced to the members of your extended family and to their relatives and friends in that order. To introduce you to your surroundings you will be shown the sun and the four corners of the building that houses you. Under your pillow certain paraphernalia will be placed - charms, a talisman, or some sort of prayer to protect you. Your umbilical cord is buried in the ground near the place where you are born. This, it is believed, will protect you and link you to your birthplace.

Relatives and friends will wish to know what to call you and will ask what your name means if they are not already familiar with it. If for some reason your parents have not decided in advance on your real name, the name that you will grow with and use for the rest of your life, *jina la ukubwani*, they will bestow on you a childhood name, *jina la utotoni*. This temporary name is a sort of affectionate nickname.

On the fortieth day both you and your mother will have a ritual wash to purify both of you and end your first uncertain period of life. Regardless of the changes modernity has brought, because of the high rate of child mortality in the first month after birth that used to be common, a traditional rite is still performed. Another sunna, or tradition established by the Prophet MuHammad, is to perform an *'aqiiqa*, the slaughtering of an animal, usually a small sheep, to celebrate the birth of a baby. This is accompanied by shaving or cutting the baby's hair to stimulate its growth. This is known as *Irtihaan bil'aqiiqa*. The root *'iqqa* means 'the hair of a fetus,' a pledge made with *'aqiiqa* for the life of the baby against the *shayTaan*, the devil. The meat of the slaughtered animal is distributed among relatives and friends. Some people collect all the bones of the slaughtered animal and carefully bury them, in the belief that this will protect the bones of the child from breaking. *'Aqiiqa* may take place any time within two years of the baby's birth. Opinions differ on how soon it should take place but the sooner the better. On this occasion your parents will distribute *sadaka*, alms, in your name and for your further protection. If you are a boy you will be circumcised preferably before the age of seven and not later than eleven. This may be done with or without ceremony and celebration. Girls do not undergo circumcision among Muslim Waswahili.[3]

In some regions of Africa naming ceremonies are very elaborate and extensive. They include employing a religious teacher (*mu'allim* in Arabic, *mallam, malam* or *malama* in Hausa-Fulani, *m'allim* or *mwalimu* in Kiswahili) to recite special prayers during the ceremony and many animals are sacrificed. Not all these rituals are explicitly prescribed by the Islamic religion.[4] They reflect the easy alliance of Islam and local African customs and traditions, handed down through the ages.

A newborn child is important in any family but in Islamic society the importance of the newborn is signified by the name bestowed on the infant. A child's first or given name is the beginning of a very special education. First,the child learns that without question he or she is loved. This is expressed in the Arabic proverb:

Al-qird fii 'ayni ummihi ghazaal.

A monkey in his mother's eyes is a gazelle.

The child's knowledge of self starts with the name. Then, as the child grows and develops, other dimensions of importance to identity, age, gender, kinship, physical characteris-

15

tics, friends and education become relevant. But nothing is more important than liking one's name as a child.

African parents choose their child's first name (the given name) with great care. They hope to confer on the child the attributes associated with the name and to convey a message to all who hear it. Some people believe that a name may actually contribute to a child's growth of character and development. A disapproval of an action by the child is often instantly interpolated with a reminder to his name: in Kiswahili *'Jina limemdhuru'* the name has let him down. The name is believed to influence a child's self-perception. I once heard a four-year-old child whose mother was reprimanding him by calling him 'Boy' remind her that his name was *SulTaan*, the ruler! He took the meaning of his name more seriously than his mother.

Names have historical and ethical dimensions. A newborn has many names reconstructed from his family's lineage as far back as anyone can remember through the father's line. A boy, for example, might be known as *Ibrahim bin* (son of) *MuHammed bin Ibrahim bin Ahmed Al-Zinjjy*. This for example, is how a teacher in the classroom can distinguish between the three *MuHammeds* of one generation. Often he will use only the first three names. Yet none are more important than the first, his own, name because that was chosen just for him and sanctified by ritual. The child's last name or surname is his patrilineal, clan or tribal name.

Ibrahim's sister in this patrilineal society might be named *Fatma bint* (daughter of) *MuHammed bin Ibrahim bin Ahmed al-Zinjjy*. Note that only the first name *FaTma* indicates gender. The rest of the names she bears are those of her father, grandfather, great grandfather and clan or tribe. Women's names more often are left out of clan genealogies. The only time a person is given the mother's name is at one's funeral rites. The reason being the mother's identity is irrefutable. In life since lineage descent is traced through the male line (patrilineage), it is through patrilineage that every member is able to preserve and maintain his cultural heritage and values. A child learns what it means to belong.

A child should always be given a positive personal name. A child's right to have a beautiful name is a basic right. How successful this is as a way of training a child for life in society is a study worth further research.

NAMES AND REPUTATIONS

Understandably then in an Islamic society one's reputation is linked with one's given name. A person of good reputation is described as having a good name and when he dies he is said to leave behind a good name. In some African languages such as Manika the very word for a name, *togo*, means both given name and reputation. For the Hausa the word *suna* means both name and tradition. In Kigala a name is *mekka* and naming is *mekka base* signifying the sacredness of the name to this society. Mecca is a sacred place to the Muslims. In Swahili the word for name, *jina*, is used to identify a person to show who he or she is. In Arabic the word for name, *ism*, means both name and reputation.

Nevertheless, once given in a name, a reputation develops through one's own initiative. Without the growth of a good reputation the meaning of a person's name has no significance. A name speaks or does not speak for itself. An Egyptian proverb proclaims:

Ism bilaa jism.

A name without a body, that is without a reality.

The Swahili say:

Jina tu.

It's only a name; the object is not worth its name.

The first meaning of a name was chosen and bestowed by loving parents. The child had no say in its selection. The growing child learns what it signifies as he or she grows up and likes or dislikes it. But in African society, you have to live with the name you are given for names are not easy to change. Nevertheless you do have control over the reputation of your given name, the dignity that goes with it. The famous East African poet Shaaban Robert Ufukwe delights in dwelling on the importance of good reputation in several of his poems. He has even written a poem called *Jina, The Name*. The first verse reads:

Mtu wa fikira njema kwa watu huacha jina,

A thoughtful person lives behind his name,

Na watu wajao nyuma wakapenda kuliona,

And those who come after him would cherish it,

Katika dunia nzima likawa kubwa hazina,

And it is treasured throughout the world,

Na akili si kusema lakini ni kufikiri,

And the wisdom contained lies not in speaking but in thinking,

Kwa kujua jambo jema lisilokuwa na shari.

in knowing something perfect.[5]

Shaaban is referring to one's reputation: the privilege, honor and distinction that one acquires through learning and thinking in order to be well remembered after one's death. Reputation comes from behavior and character, abilities and achievements, and participation in and contribution to the community.

This reputation sometimes triggers a nickname from one's peers which may be good or bad. It may relate to a physical abnormality or a peculiar characteristic. An individual may be aware of his nickname if he is addressed by it or if it is an unkind one he may be unaware of it.

The Qur'aan instructs a Muslim not to call another person by an abusive name.[6] This should remind parents of the importance of being sensitive to their children's feelings and self-esteem. Children learn and thrive on praise, encouragement and objective criticism not by being abused, reproached, put down and denigrated.

FORMS OF ADDRESS

During a life time, a man or woman may acquire several names. Adults, for example, are not usually addressed by their given names by any one younger than they. In public, husbands and wives rarely use each other's given names but substitute instead *teknonyms* such as *mama*, mother of or *baba*, father of, or *binti*, daughter of or, *ukhti*, sister instead. A younger person usually addresses an elder with a relationship term such as mother, father, aunt, uncle, grandfather, grandmother, sister and brother. Even when there is no kinship, older friends of the family are addressed in this respectful way. It is considered disrespectful for a young person to address someone older than himself without a title, such as in Kiswahili *Bwana, Bibi, Siti, Mwana, Baba, Mama, Dada, Da* or *Kaka*.

According to one tradition, the Prophet MuHammad declared:

He is not of us who is not merciful to our younger people, and does not honor the old among us.

Kindness and respect go together and are essential in any family and society. Mother- and father-in-laws are referred to as mother and father or aunt and uncle. A brother- or sister-in-law may also be referred to as a brother- or sister-in-law, as *shemeji* in Kiswahili. Avoidance of the use of one's real names is also associated with the power of the word and the fear of magic. The tabu of not using a person's name and using an alternative one, a euphemism, be it a nickname, epithet, relational term or a term of endearment, has been discussed by many scholars.

NOTES

1. For Arabic speakers there are many to choose from but non-Arabic parents have a limited number to choose from and include those l list in the References.
2. See Zawawi, 1993, pp.7-10 for examples relating to Waswahili.
3. In some African societies such as the Maasai unmarried women undergo a clitoridectomy, a feminine equivalent of circumcision but it is not a Muslim custom.
4. For instance the custom of circumcising a child is pre-Islamic.
5. Shaaban Robert, *Diwani ya Shaaban 6 Kielezo cha Fasihi*, Thomas Nelson and Sons, 1968, p.51. The translation is mine.
6. See below on Abusive Names.

CHAPTER THREE

MUSLIM NAMES

SOURCE AND SIGNIFICANCE

To understand the power of words and so the power of names let us learn from the words of the Qur'aan:

Alam taraa kayfa Daraba llahu mathalan kalimatan Tayyibatan kashajaratin Tayyibatin aSluhaa thaabitun wa far'uhaa fii ssamaa'i.
Tu'tii ukulahaa kulla Hiinin bi'idhni rabbihaa wa yaDribu llaahu l-amthaala li-nnaasi la'allahum yatad-hakkaruun.
Wa mathalu kalimatin khabiythatin kashajaratin khabiythati ijtuththat min fawqi-l-arDi maa-lahaa min qaraar.

Have you not seen how God constructs a parable out of a good word, like a good tree, whose root is firm and its branches reach into heaven?
Giving its fruit at every season by the will of its Lord?
God coins parables for mankind so that human beings may reflect on them.
A parable constructed out of a bad word is like a rotten tree pulled out of the ground, it lacks stability.[1]

The power of words has long attracted the attention of African theologians and philosophers. Islamic teaching is explicit on the need for and relevance of a name for every animate and inanimate substance. The names of God are said to be beautiful names: *lahu -lasmaa'-l-Husnaa*.[2]

The Qur'aan tells us that God taught Adam names:

wa 'allama Aadama l-asmaa'a kullahaa thumma 'araDahum 'alaa -l-malaa'ikati faqaala anbi'unii biasmaai haa'ulaai in kuntum Saadiqiin.
qaaluu subHanaka laa 'ilma lanaa illaa maa 'allamtanaa innaka anta -l-'aliimu -l-Hakiim.

And He taught Adam all the names of everything, then showed them to the angels, saying: Tell me the names of these if you are right.

They said: Glory be to God; we have no knowledge except whatever You have taught us. You are the Knowing, the Wise.[3]

And in another verse, God said:

qaala yaa Aadamu anbi'hum biasmaaihim falammaa anba'a hum biasmaaihim qaala alam aqul lakum innii a'lamu ghayba ssamawaati wa-larDi wa a'lam maa tubduuna wa maa kuntum taktumuun.

O Adam! Inform them of their names, and when he had informed them of their names, He said: Did I not tell you that I know the secret of the heavens and the earth? And I know that which you disclose and which you hide.[4]

The first thing to note here is the relation of Adam to his name. He is considered in Islam to be the first human being on earth, the father of all as well as a prophet. His name in Arabic and in the Qur'aan signifies 'a person' in the singular and its plural is *awaadum* 'people' in some dialects.[5] The word Aadam also means earth. Adam stands for the archetype of humanity, the first and original person.

There is a second thing to note. The first lesson God teaches Adam is the name of every animate and inanimate thing. Thus Adam is given the knowledge and ability to identify all God's creations and to name them. This is what his intellect and power are based on: his knowledge of names.

BAD OR ABUSIVE NAMES

The Qur'aan strongly condemns the use of any derogatory names.

> yaa ayyuha lladhiina aamanuu laa yaskhar qawmun min qawmin 'asaa an yakuunuu khayran minhum wa laa nisaaun min nisaain 'asaa an yakunna khayran minhunna wa laa talmizuu anfusakum wa laa tanaabazuu bil-alqaabi bi'sa l-ismu lfusuuqu ba'da l-iiymaani wa man lam yatub faulaa'ika humu ZZaalimuuna.

> You who believe let no man deride another who may be better than he, let no woman deride another who may be better than she. Neither defame one another, nor insult one another by bad nicknames. It is bad to use an abusive name instead of one you can believe in. Those who do not turn away from such a practice are wrongdoers.[6]

I don't know any Muslim parents who call their child Iblis, (Satan), *Fir'awn* (Pharaoh), *Hamaan*,[7] *ShayTaan* or *Jinn*, (Devil), *'Aduu* (Enemy), *Khinziir* (Pig), *Himaar* (Donkey) or *Kalb* (Dog). The last three were actually used by Arabs to name their children in the *Jaahiliyya*, the period of ignorance, but this is utterly contrary to the Islamic idea that a name or *ism* should exalt an individual and raise him to his Creator.[8]

IN THE NAME OF GOD

A Muslim is taught from early childhood the importance of calling on the name of God.

> Bismi-llaahi-r-RaHmaani-r-RaHiim.

In the name of God (the One), the Compassionate, the Merciful.

These words *In the name of God*, an invocation, open every chapter in the Qur'aan[9] The phrase is written in talismans and amulets, on personal ornaments and is inscribed over doors for protection. It is also a prayer that is uttered whenever one embarks on something new. The naming of the Creator bestows the power to act; it gives control over a situation and the courage to face it. A child first learns the phrase when he begins his meal.

The very first *aya* (verse) of the Revelation of the Qur'aan is:

iqra' Bismi Rabbika lladhii khalaq,
khalaqa l-insaana min 'alaq.
iqra' wa rabbuka l-akram
lladhii 'allama bi-lqalam.
'allama l-insaana maa lam ya'lam.

Recite in the name of your Lord who created,
Created man from a clot of blood.
Recite and it is your Lord the most Generous
Who taught by the pen.
Taught man that which he knew not.[10]

Or again:

wa qaala rkabuu fiiha bismillaahi majraaha
wa mursaahaa
inna rabbii laghafuuru rraHiim.

And he said: Embark therein. In the name of God be its course and its mooring. Indeed! my Lord is Forgiving,   Merciful.[11]

God's name encompasses the assurance and strength of what is to be done. It imparts the Islamic consciousness of the image of God in everything. The misuse and abuse of the invocation by evil magicians and others has become a common theme in recent Muslim stories and films.[12]

GOD'S NAME - ALLAH

The name Allah, the greatest Name to all Muslims is derived from I-l-h. When the middle vowels are added to the root it becomes *Ilaah* as in.

illaahu-kum ilaahu-n waHidu-n.

Your God is one[13].

or: laa Ilaaha illa llah.

There is no other God but the One God.

When the definite article is added to *Ilaah* it becomes *al-ilaah*. In some grammatical contexts when the definite article is added it changes the phrase *al-Ilaah* to *Allah*. The name is constructed around the Unity and Oneness of the Divine, the absolute power, the universal creating force. Identified by any name, He is the Creator, the One.[14]

Many Muslims like to name their children *'Abd-Allah*. The worshipper of Allah. Prophet MuHammad was the first to be endowed with this name:

wa annahu lammaa qaama 'abdullaahi yad'uuhu kaaduu yakuunuuna 'alayhi libadaa.

And when *'Abdu Allah* (the servant of God) stood up to appeal to Him, they crowded on him, almost stifling.[15]

The name Allah is never used as a personal name without being combined with another word such as *'abd*, a worshipper of.[16] Thus *'abdu+Allah* becomes *'abd+Allah 'Abdallah* or *Abdullah*. In the literature this sometimes appears as two separate words *Abd+ Allah*, i.e. *Abd Allah*. The Qur'aan calls on Man to worship the Creator.

wa lillaahi yasjudu maa fii s-samaawaati wa maa fii larDi min daabatin wa l-malaaikati wa hum laa yastakbiruun.[17]

Whatever is in Heaven and whatever is on Earth

bows down before God, whether they are animals or angels, and they supplicate themselves.

Since everything belongs to God and man is part of God's universe, he is associated with God. No wonder then that this is the most used name among Muslims.[18] Its meaning connects the person with God, he is *'Abdullah*, the worshipper of God. Many other words may be combined with the name Allah. For example:

Aayatullah	God's sign
'AbbaadAllah	God's worshipper
Amaanullah	God's trust
Amrullah	God's decree
Asadullah	God's lion
'ATaa'llah	God's gift
'ATfullah	God's affection
'Awnullah	God's help
'Azizullah	God's beloved
Baabullah	God's door
Badii'ullah	God's marvel
Barakatullah	God's blessings
Basmalla	God's name
Beitallah	God's house
Daf'ullah	God's defense
FaDlullah	God's graciousness
Fakhrullah	God's glory
Farjallah	God's comfort
FatHallah	God's victory
Habibullah	God's beloved

Hamdullah	God's praise
Hamidullah	God's praiser
Hasbullah	God's reckoning
Hibbatullah	God's gift
Hidaayatullah	God's reward
Hubbullah	God's love
Hudaallah	God's guidance
Hujjatullah	God's proof
'Inaayatullah	God's manifestation
Jaabullah	God's answer
Jaadullah	God's result
Jaarullah	God's charge
Khaliilullah	God's friend
Khayrullah	God's best
LaTiifullah	God's grace
Maashaa'allah	God's wishes
Minnatullah	God's blessing
MuHibbullah	God's love
Najiibullah	God's eminence
NaSrullah	God's victory
Ni'matullah	God's grace
Nuurullah	God's light
RaHmatullah	God's compassion
Rizqullah	God's sustenance
Sa'dullah	God's help
Safiyyullah	God's chosen
Salamullah	God's peace
San'ullah	God's creation
Sayfullah	God's sword
Shafii'ullah	God's mediator
Shahidullah	God's witness
Sharii'atullah	God's way
Shukrullah	God's praise
Taqiillah	God's fear
Thanaaullah	God's appreciation

'Ubaydullah	God's worshipper
Ummatullah	God's community
Waliyyullah	God's friend
Ziyaadat-allah	God's abundance

The name Allah appears in other combinations and formulae and is heard all the time whether one is asking for protection, praising, promising, consoling or cajoling.[19] Phrases such as *Ya Allah* (O God), *Wallah* (By God), *AlHamdulillah* (Praise the Lord), *SubHaanallah* (Praise be to God), *Astaghfirullah* (I ask forgiveness from God), *Mashaa'allah* (What God's like), *Inshaa'llah* (God's will), *Jazaaka llah* (God rewards you), *Fi amaani llah* (In God's protection), *Hallahallah* (God is the reminder), *'Amrallah* (In the name of God), *Amrallah* (God's decree), *'aDakallah* (May God compensate you), *Juwarballah* (God forbid) punctuate Muslims' daily conversations, spicing their ideas, verifying and vouching for their intentions. The inspiration for this comes from the Qur'aan which calls upon Muslims not to say that they *will* do something without mentioning God's name:

> wa laa taquulanna lishay'in innii faa'ilun dhaalika ghadan. illa an yashaa'a llahu wadhkur rabbaka idhaa nasiita wa qul 'asaa an yahdiyani rabbii liaqraba min hadhaa rashadan.

> And don't say of anything: Surely I will do it tomorrow. Unless God pleases; and remember your Lord when you forget and say: Maybe my Lord will steer me to a course nearer to the truth than this.[20]

THE BEAUTIFUL NAMES

A verse in the Qur'aan refers to the use of God's beautiful names:

wa lillaahi -l-asmaa'-l-Husnaa fad'uu bihaa
wa dharuu lladhiina yulHiduuna fii asmaa'ihi
sayujzawna maa kaanuu ya'maluun.

God has the finest names, therefore call on Him by them and leave alone those who violate the sanctity of His names; they will be judged for whatever they have been doing.[21]

Al-Asmaa'a-l-Husnaa (the most beautiful names), refer to Allah's many qualities and many powers. Muslims are urged to remember and use ninety-nine of these names, to call on Him using them, and to call one another by them.[22] The attributes of God are also used as personal names in combination with the word *'abdu*, worshipper/servant of. One example is *'Abdu-al-RaHmaan* pronounced *'abdurraHmaan'*, the worshipper of the Merciful One.

Al-Asmaa'a-l'Husnaa, the most beautiful names, recommend desirable human characteristics for emulation. Although parents giving them to their offspring have ninety-nine attributes to choose from, some are more popular than others. A note on pronunciation accompanies the list that follows.

The ninety-nine attributes of God are:

Attribute	Meaning	Pronunciation
Al-raHman	the Compassionate	ArraHmaan
Al-raHiim	the Merciful	ArraHiim
Al-malik	the King	Almalik
Al-qudduus	the Pure and Holy	Alqudduus
Al-salaam	the Savior	Assalaam
Al-mu'min	the Inspirer	Almu'min
Al-muhaymin	the Guardian	Almuhaymin
Al-'aziiz	the Precious	Al'aziiz

Al-jabbaar	the Courageous	Aljabbaar
Al-mutakabbir	the Greatest	Almutakabbir
Al-khaaliq	the Creator	Alkhaaliq
Al-baari'	the Orderer	Albaari'
Al-musawwir	the Shaper	Almusawwir
Al-ghaffaar	the Forgiving	Alghaffaar
Al-qahaar	the Conquerer, Subduer	Alqahaar
Al-wahhaab	the Giver	Alwahhaab
Al-razzaaq	the Sustainer	Arrazaaq
Al-fattaah	the Opener	Alfattaah
Al-'aliim	the Knower	Al'aliim
Al-qaabid	the Holder	Alqaabid
Al-baasit	the Reliever	Albaasit
Al-khaafiD	the Restricter	AlkhaafiD
Al-raafi'	the Raiser	Arraafi'
Al-mu'izz	the Honorer	Almu'izz

Al-mudhdhil	the Subduer	Almudhdhil
Al-samii'	the Hearer	Assamii'
Al-basiir	the Seer	Albasiir
Al-hakam	the Judge	Alhakam
Al-'adl	the Just	Al'adl
Al-latiif	the Gentle	Allatiif
Al-khabiir	the Aware	Alkhabiir
Al-haliim	the Gentle	Alhaliim
Al'aziim	the Great	Al'aziim
Al-ghafuur	the Forgiver	Alghafuur

Al-shakuur	the Rewarder	Ashshakuur
Al-'alii	the Highest	Al'alii
Al-kabiir	the Greatest	Alkabiir
Al-haafiz	the Preserver	Alhaafiz
Al-muqiit	the Nourisher	Almuqiit
Al-hasiib	the Accounter	Alhasiib
Al-jaliil	the Mighty	Aljaliil
Al-kariim	the Generous	Alkariim
Ar-raqiib	the Watchful	Arraqiib
Al-mujiib	the Responder	Almujiib
Al-waasi'	the Magnanimous	Alwaasi'
Al-hakiim	the Wise	Alhakiim
Al-waduud	the Loving	Alwadfuud
Al-maajid	the Majestic	Almaajid
Al-baa'ith	the Resurrector	Albaa'ith
Al-shahiid	the Witness	Ashshahiid
Al-haqq	the Truth	Alhaqq
Al-wakiil	the Trustee	Alwakiil
Al-qawii	the Strong	Alqawii
Al-matiin	the Forceful	Almatiin
Al-waliyyu	the Protector	Alwaliyyu
Al-haamid	the Praised	Alhaamid
Al-muhsii	the Appropriator	Almuhsii
Al-mubdi'	the Originator	Almubdi'
Al-mu'iid	the Restorer	Almu'iid
Al-muhyi	the Nourisher	Almuhyi
Al-mumiit	the Taker of Life	Almumiit
Al-hayy	the Living	Alhayy
Al-qayyuum	the Eternal	Alqayyuum
Al-waajid	the Finder	Alwaajid
Al-maajid	the Glorious	Almaajid
Al-waahid	the Only One	Alwaahid
Al-samad	the Eternal	Assamad
Al-qaadir	the Able, Powerful	Alqaadir
al-muqtadir	the Creator of Power	Almuqtadir

Al-muqaddim	the Expediter	Almuqaddim
Al-mu'akhkhir	the Delayer	Almuakhkhir
Al-awwal	the First	Alawwal
Al-aakhir	the Last	Alaakhir
Al-zaahir	the Manifest	Azzahir
Al-baatin	the Hidden	Albaatin
Al-waalii	the Governor	Alwaalii
Al-muta'aalii	the Supreme	Almuta'aalii
Al-barr	the Doer of Good	Al-barr
Al-tawwaab	the Guide to Repentance	Attawaab
Al-muntaqim	the Avenger	Almuntaqim
Al-'afuwu	the Forgiver	Al'afuww
Al-rauuf	the Kind	Arrauuf
Maliku-al-mulk	the Owner of All	Malikulmulk
Dhu-l-jalaali	the Lord of Majesty	Dhuljalaali
wa-l-ikraam	and Bounty	walikraam
Al-muqsit	the Equitable	Almuqsit
Al-jaami'	the Gatherer	Aljaami'
Al-ghanii	the Self Sufficient	Alghanii
Al-mughnii	the Enricher	Almughnii
Al-maani'	the Preventer of Harm	Almaani'
Aldarr	the Creator of Harm	Addarr
Al-naafi'	the Beneficent	Annaafi'
Al-nuur	the Light	Annuur
Al-haadii	the Guide	Alhaadii
Al-badii'	the Originator	Albadii'
Al-baaqii	the Everlasting	Albaaqii
Al-waarith	the Inheritor	Alwaarith
Al-rashiid	the Righteous	Arrashii
Al-sabuur	the Patient	Assabuur

The image we conjure from these qualities are:

1. God is Creator of all: the king, the greatest, the magnanimous, mighty, first and the last, judge, holy, savior, forceful, just, trust, restorer, fighter and friend.

2. God is compassionate: merciful, forgiver, giver, nourisher, sustainer, reliever, holder, generous, merciful, gentle and loving

3. God is organizer: orderer, doer, watcher, listener, seer, responder, protector, appropriator, inspirer and rewarder.

These attributes inculcate ethical values. When they are used as personal names they are preceded by the expression *Abdu-l-* (the worshipper/servant of). Thus, for example, a child is named *Abdulkhaaliq* (the worshipper of the Creator), *Abduljabbaar* (the worshipper of the Courageous one), *Abdulaziim* (the worshipper of the Great one) and *Abdurrahmaan* (the worshipper of the Compassionate one) and so on.[23] Most of these names express qualities that are expected of all human beings: kindness, truthfulness, goodness, honesty, faithfulness, courage, justice and the like. Muslims memorize these attributes and recite them frequently following their daily prayers. Through the names, moral values are brought into our daily discourse reminding us of the ethical relationships they entail. A well known tradition quotes Prophet MuHammad as saying:

> innakum tad'uuna yawma l-qiyaamati biasmaaikum wa biasmaai abaaikum, faHsanuu asmaa'kum.

> You will be called by your names and your fathers' names on the day of judgment so choose beautiful names.

The Prophet describes the best names as:

> Khayru-l-asmaa' maa Hamida wa 'abada.

> The best of names are those that praise and worship.

Another tradition attributed to the Prophet is:

The best of your names are Abdullah, the worshipper of God and AbdurraHmaan the worshipper of the Merciful.

The Prophet is said to have left a number of sunnas or aHadiith (oral traditions) emphasizing that children should be given good names and names that recall God. To him the most beautiful names are those that relate one to God and his attributes. He is said to have changed names such as *Huzn* (rough, sadness) to *Sahal* (ease), *ZaHm* (hustle) to *Bashiir* (predictor of good tidings), *Nushba* (fierceness, meddler) to *'Utba* (hesitant, censors) and *'AaSiya* (rebellious) to *Jamiila* (beautiful). To him the worst names are *Harb* (war,enmity) and *Murrah* (bitterness) and these two are to be avoided. These were names Arabs used during the period of *al-jaahiliyya*, the period of ignorance, before his prophesy.

Not all the Beautiful Names are used in naming girls. Those that are require the addition of a feminine suffix. The meaning and pronunciation of the following examples are the same as those for male names:

'Adla/'Adlah	'Afuwa
'Aliya	'Aziiza
'AZiima	BaSiira
Ghafuura	Ghaniyya
Haadiya	HaafiZa/HafiiZa
Haamida	Haasiba
Hakiima	Jaliila
Kariima	Khabiira
LaTiifa	Maajida
Malika	Muhaymina
Muluuka	Naafi'a
Ni'ma	Qudsiyya
RaHiima	RaHma

Raqiiba	Rashiida
Raufa	Sabuura
Salaama	Shakuura
WaHiida	Zaahira

NAMES SIGNIFYING THE WORSHIP OF GOD

The word *'abdu* 'worship' combines with an attribute to form a given name and relates the children to worshipping their Creator, the Almighty. Another word that is used extensively in conveying the same idea is the word *diin* 'religion' or 'faith.' With the noun added, the word *diin* produces many boys' names. For example:

'Afiifuddiin	The uprighteousness of the faith
Akmaluddiin	The perfection of the faith
'Alaa'ddiin	The nobility of the faith
Amaanuddiin	The peace of the faith
Amiinuddiin	The security of the faith
Amiruddiin/Amruddiin	The power of the faith
Asaduddiin	The bravery of the faith
Athiiruddiin	The nobleness of the faith
'Awnuddiin	The help of the faith
Badruddiin	The crescent of the faith
Bahaauddiin	The beauty of the faith
Bahiiruddiin	The dazzle of the faith
Bashiiruddiin	The predictor of the faith
Burhanuddiin	The proof of the faith
Diyaa'ddiin	The glow of the faith
Fakhruddiin	The glory of the faith
Falakuddiin	The star of the faith
Fariduddin	The excellence of the faith
FarraHuddiin	The joy of the faith
FatHuddiin	The victory of the faith
Fawzuddiin	The success of the faith
Ghiyaathuddiin	The abundance of the faith

Hamiduddiin	The praiser of the faith
'Imaaduddiin	The pillar of the faith
Imaamuddin	The leader of the faith
'Izzuddiin	The power of the faith
Jalaaluddin	The glory of the faith
Jamaaluddiin	The beauty of the faith
Kalimuddiin	The discourse of the faith
Kamaluddiin	The perfection of the faith
Khayruddiin	The best of the faith
Lisaanuddiin	The voice of the faith
Majduddiin	The diligence of the faith
Muhadhdhibuddiin	The disciplined of the faith
MuHyyiddiin	The sustainer of the faith
Mu'iinuddiin	The helper of the faith
Mu'izzuddiin	The respector of the faith
Mujaahiduddiin	The defender of the faith
MuSliHuddiin	The reformer of the faith
NaaSiruddiin	The savior of the faith
Najiibuddiin	The noble of the faith
Najmuddiin	The star of the faith
NaSir-ddiin	The savior of the faith
NiZaamuddiin	The harmony of the faith
Nuruddiin	The light of the faith
NuSratuddiin	The help of the faith
Qamaruddiin	The moon of the faith
Qiwaamuddiin	The strength of the faith
Saafi-ddiin	The pure of the faith
SabaaHuddiin	The beauty of the faith
Sadruddiin	The leader of the faith
Sa'duddiin	The good fortune of the faith
SalaaHuddin	The righteousness of the faith
Sayfuddiin	The sword of the faith
Shamsuddiin	The sun of the faith
Sharafuddiin	The noble of the faith
Shihaabuddiin	The shooting star of the faith

Sinaanuddiin	The spearhead of the faith
Siraajuddiin	The lamp of the faith
Taajuddiin	The crown of the faith
Taqiyyuddiin	The devoutness of the faith
Wariithuddin	The inheritor of the faith
Zahruddiin	The blossom of the faith
Za'iimuddiin	The leader of the faith
Zakiyyuddiin	The integrity of the faith
Zaynuddiin	The beauty of the faith

These names encourage positive attitudes. Negativeness or abusive behavior is not encouraged.[24]

THE NAMES OF PROPHETS

Muslims like to use the names of the twenty-five prophets mentioned in the Qur'aan. These are listed below along with their Biblical equivalents:

Muslim	Biblical
Adam	Adam
Al-Yas'a	Elisha
Ayyub	Job
Da'ud	David
Dhulkifl	Ezekiel
Harun	Aaron
Huud	
Ibrahim	Abraham
Idriis	Enoch
Ilyaas	Elyas/Elias
'Isaa	Jesus
IsHaaq	Isaac
Ismaa'iil	Ishmael/Samuel
LuuT	Lot
MuHammad	Muhammad
Musa	Moses

37

NuH	Noah
SaleH	
Shu'ayb	Jethro
Sulaymaan	Solomon
Yahya	John
Ya'quub	Jacob
Yunus	Jonah
Yusuf	Joseph
Zakariyya	Zachariah/Zakariah

THE NAMES OF PROPHET MUḤAMMAD

The very name of Prophet MuHammad itself generates
names that are inherited by Muslims. They are names with
meanings as well as relational significance. They include:

'Aadil	just
Abal-Qaasim	one who divides fairly
AHmad	praiseworthy
Amiin	trustworthy
Bashiir	predictor
Haadii	leader
Haamid	grateful
Haashir	assemble
Habiib	dear one
Hakiim	wise
Jawaad	generous
Khaatim	the last one
Khaliil	friend
Mahdii	reformer
MaHmuud	praiseworthy
Ma'muun	trustworthy
ManSuur	victorious
Mubashshir	predictor
Mukhtaar	chosen
Muniir	brilliant

MuSliH	reformer
MuSTafaa	chosen[25]
Mutawakkil	one who depends on God
Nabii	proclaimer
Nadhiir	consecrated to God, preacher
Rasuul	messenger
Saadiq	truthful
Sayyid	master
Shaahid	witness
Shahiid	witness
Siraaj	light
Tayyib	good

What image of the Prophet do these qualities convey? He is trustworthy, praiseworthy, gracious, generous, tolerant, just, brilliant, a reformer, guide and messenger, qualities that deserve emulation. According to one Prophetic tradition, a father has three obligations toward his son: to teach him to write, to select a good name for him, and to arrange his marriage when he comes of age.

In one of his sermons *Imam 'Ali ibn Abi Talib*[26] is said to have stated:

Allah deputed the Prophet with light, and accorded him the highest precedence in selection. Through him Allah united those who were divided, overpowered the powerful, overcame difficulties and levelled rugged ground. He thus removed misguidance from right and left.[27]

NAMES OF PROPHET MUHAMMAD'S FAMILY

The names of several immediate members of the Prophet's family are also used as given names. These include:
His mother:

Aamina bint Wahab

His father:

'Abdallah bin 'Abd-l-MuTTalib

His grandfather:

'Abd-al-MuTTalib ibn Hashim bin 'Abd-Manaaf bin QuSSay

His wives[28]:

Khadija bint Khuwaylid
Sawda bint Zu'ma bin Qays
Zaynab bint Khuzaymah
Umm Salma, Hind bint Abi Umayya bin Al-Mughyra
'Aisha bint Abii Bakar
Hafsa bint 'Umar bin Al-KhaTTaab
Safiyya bint Hayy bin AkhTab[29]
Zaynab bint JaHsh Al-Asadiyya
Umm Habiiba, Ramla bint Abi Sufyaan bin Harb
Jawayriyya bint Al-Haarith Al-Khazaa'iyya
Maymuuna bint Al-Haarith bin Hazn

Two others, Asmaa' bint Al-Nu'maan Al-Kindiyya and 'Amra bint Yaziid Al-Kalbiyya, he divorced before consummating the marriage.

His daughters :

Zaynab
Ruqayya
Umm Kulthuum
FaaTima

His uncles:

Al-'Abbaas
Abu-Taalib

His aunt:

Arwa bint AHmed bin Ja'far

His cousins:

'Ali and his sons: al-Hasan and al-Husayn and Hamza

His sister by sharing her mother's milk:

Shaymaa' bint Al-Haarith

The names of several famous Muslim women are also given to newborn children. These include:

Asmaa	the daughter of Abuu Bakar
Bilqiis	the Queen of Saba', Shiba,
Sheba or	Sheeba
Haajar or Aajar	the mother of the Prophet Isma'iil
Haliima	the woman who fostered Prophet MuHammad after the death of his mother
Hawaa'	Eve
Maryam	Mary
Rabii'a	the mystic woman from Al-Basra who lived around A.D.717-801
Saara	the wife of Ibrahiim
Sukayna	the daughter of Al-Husayn
Zubayda or Zubeida	the wife of Haaruun Rashiid

41

The personal names of Prophet Muhammad's Khalifas (successors to the caliphate) are also given to male children. These are :

Abu-Bakar Siddiq (A.D. 632-634)
'Umar ibn-l-KhaTTaab (A.D.634-644)
'Uthmaan ibn 'affaan (A.D.644-656)
'Ali ibn Abii Taalib (A.D.656-661)

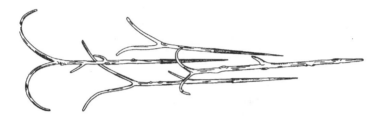

The names of several other kinsmen or *sahaaba* (companions) of the Prophet are also used. These include:

Bilaal ibn RabaaH	the first Muadhdhin (muazzin) to call Muslims to prayer. He was an African
Zaaid ibn Thaabit	the Prophet's adopted son
Zaynul-'aabidiin	the grandson of 'Ali, Prophet MuHammad's cousin and his grandson
Ja'far ibn Abii Taalib	a cousin of Prophet MuHammad

Muslims also use the names of the *Shi'a Imaams* (leaders) for newborn boys. These include:

Ali ibn Abi-Taalib   (A.D. 632 - 661)
Al-Hasan ibn 'Ali   (A.D. 662 - 669)
Al-Husayn Husayn ibn 'Ali (A.D. 670 - 680)
'Ali Hussein Sajjad

(Zayn-Al-'Aabidin)	(A.D. 681 - 711/2)
MuHammad Al-Baaqir	(A.D. 711 - 731)
Ja'far Al-Saadiq	(A.D. 732 - 765)
Muusa Al-KaaZim	(A.D. 766 - 799)
'Alii Al-RiDaa/'Ali al-Reza	(A.D. 780 - 818)
MuHammad Taqi/al-Jawaad	(A.D. 819 - 835)
'Ali Al-Haadi/ Al-Naqi	(A.D. 834 - 868)
Al-Hasan Al-'Askari	(A.D. 869 - 874)
Muhammad Al-MuntaZar/Al-Mahdi	(A.D. 875 - 878)

NAMES DERIVED FROM VERSES
IN THE QUR'AAN

Many other names used by Arab Muslims and non-Arab
Muslims alike are derived from chosen verses in the Qur'aan.
Each sura (chapter) in the Qur'aan has a name or a title and
a number. Out of the total of 114 suras twenty-five of the
titles are also personal names. These are:
'imraan, Yunus, Hud, Yusuf, Ibraahiim, Maryam, Taaha, Al-
Hajj, Al-Nuur, Luqmaan, Saba', Yaa Siin, Al-Mu'min,
MuHammad, Al-Najm, Al-Qamar, Al-RaHmaan, A-Jumu'a,
NuuH, Al-Muzammil, Al-Taariq, Al-Shams, Al-Bayyina, Al-
Kauthar, and Al-NaSr.

The suras are connected with people whose names
then are used or with events. Four of these, *Maryam, Saba',*
Bayyina and *Kauthar*, are names of girls and the rest are for
boys. Nine of the masculine names may be given a feminine
suffix to use for girls.

The girl's name *Kauthar* comes from the first verse
and title of a sura that reads:

inn a'Taynaaka-l-Kauthar.

We have given you plenty.[30]

The word *kauthar* here means plenty but it also refers to a leg-
endary river in Paradise. In a similar fashion the boy's name
Taaha is the title and a one-word first verse of another sura.[31]

Another boy's name, *Yaasiin*, is the title and beginning verse of another sura[32] and is said to mean Man. The title of another, *Al-Muzammil* means wrapped in clothes or bundled up and this has inspired a name that may be given to both boys and girls, *Mzammil* for a boy and *Mzamiluu* for a girl. The word *zamiil* means 'a friend.'[33]

One verse in the Qur'aan, I find, has been a particularly rich source of names. This is verse 160 of Suratu al-'imraan.[34] It reads:

in *yanSurukum* llaahu falaa *ghaaliba* lakum
wa in yakhdhulukum faman dha lladhii yanSurukum
min ba'dihi wa 'alaa llahi *falyatawakkali -lmu'minuun.*

If God *supports* you
none can *overcome* you,
and if God forsakes you,
who is there to support you thereafter?
On God should *believers rely.*

This one verse has given rise to four personal names:

NaaSir	supporter, helper from the root n-S-r
Ghaalib	victorious, overcome from the root gh-l-b
Tawakkal, Mutawakkil and Wakiil	have trust, rely on from the root w-k-l
Mu'min	believer, from the root a-m-n Mu'min is the singular noun of Mu'minuun.

The opening lines of this verse are often found inscribed in attractive calligraphy. One of the finest examples is to be found in the Al-Hambra Palace in Granada in southern Spain.

NAMES FROM THE ISLAMIC CALENDAR

The Islamic calendar with its months, days of the week, parts of the day and numbers has been the source of many male and female names. These include:

MuHarram	first month of the year
'Ashuur	the first ten days of the month of MuHarram
Rabii'	third and fourth months; spring
Rabii'a	girl or boy[35]
Rajab	seventh month of the year
Sha'baan	eighth month of the year
RamaDaan	ninth month of the year
Shawwaal	tenth month of the year
'Idd	a feast day[36]
al-AHad	the first day, Sunday
al-Ithnayn	the second day, Monday
al-thulathaa'/althalaatha	the third day, Tuesday
al-arbi'aa'/al-arba'a	the fourth day, Wednesday
al-khamiis	the fifth day, Thursday
al-Jum'a	the day of congregation, Friday
al-sabt	the day of rest, Saturday

Out of these seven days those used for personal names in the Arab Islamic world are:

Khamiis	Thursday	(boy)
Khamisuu		(girl)
Jum'a	Friday	(boy)
Bint Jum'a/Mwana Juma		(girl)
Sabt	Saturday	(boy)
Sebtuu		(girl)

Parts of the day that bestow names are:

DuHaa	forenoon	(boy or girl)
Fajr	dawn	(boy or girl)
SabaaH	morning	(boy or girl)
SabiiHa	morning	(girl)
Subh	morning	(boy)
Nahaar	daytime	(boy or girl)
Layla	night, wine	(girl)

Sacred places such as Makka, Madina, Tuba', Zamzam and 'Arafa or 'Arafaat in Saudi Arabia are also among names used for Muslim children. Another name is Mi'raaj, a term that expresses the Prophet MuHammad's ascent into heaven. It also means a ladder.[37]

NOTES

1. Surat Ibraahiim 14 verses 24-26.
2. See Sura 59 verse 24.
3. In Al-Baqra, Sura 2 verse 31-32.
4. The translations of the verses from the Qur'aan are from Muhammad Marmaduke Pickthall's, *The Glorious Qur'an* and A.Yusuf Ali, *The Holy Qur'an*. I have sometimes changed certain words to improve the translation. This aya appears in Sura 2 verse 33.
5. Ibid. pp.2-3. I discuss this in my previous book. A different etymology of adam is that it is dervied from the root udmat 'to mix.'
6. In Al-Hujuraat, Sura 49 verse 11.
7. Fir'awn and his minister Hamaan oppressed and killed the Israelites.
8. I also doubt that many people call their sons Saddaam 'Commotion', derived from the verb root to push, collide, or hurt unless the parents are depicting an event in their lives.
9. An exception is for suratu-ttawbaa 'Repentance or Dispensation'. This is the first verse in sura 1X Al-Tawbaa. It does not start with an invocation since it is a continuation of the previous sura on booty where the first verse invokes God's name: Baraa'atum mina-llah wa rasuulihi. Dispensation comes from God and His messenger.
10. Al-'Alaq, Sura 96 verses 1-5.

11. In Hud, Sura 11 verse 41.
12. In the Tunisian film Soltane el Medina several satiric scenes show a diviner using the expression Bismillah 'In the name of God' in performing harmful rites to her victim.
13. Al-naHl, Sura 16, verse 22.
14. God's universal message is expressed in the Qur'aan in one of its verses:

    innamaa l-mu'minuuna ikhwatun, faslihuu bayna akhawayku-mu wa ttaquu llaaha la'allakum turhamuun.

    The believers are but brothers and sisters, so reconcile your bretheren and heed God that you may find mercy.

    Sura 49 verse 10.
15. Al-jinn, Sura 72 verse 19.
16. The word 'abd is also translated as slave of.
17. Al-NaHl, Sura 16 verse 49
18. The most common Muslim female name is perhaps FaTma, the daughter of prophet MuHammad.
19. A militant Islamic party in Lebanon even calls itself Hizbullah, the party of God.
20. Al-Kahf, Sura 18 verses 23-24.
21. Al-A'raaf, Sura 7 verse 180.
22. Much has been written about the attributes of Allah. A recent book presenting a Sufi interpretation of the names is compiled by Sheikh Tosun Bayrak al-Jerrahi al-Halveti, *The Most Beautiful Names*. He discusses the symbolic meaning of each of the ninety-nine. The Sufi followers of AHmed Al-Tijani believe that one hundred names of God, including al-ism al-A'Zam, were revealed to their leader by the Prophet MuHammad, but only ninety-nine are known.
23. The consonants that are here capitalized such as H,T,S,D, and Z stand for emphatic or velarized consonants that do not appear in the English alphabet. In Arabic they are:After certain letters, e.g. r,t,d,s,S, the l of Abdul is assimilated and takes the pronunciation of that letter as in 'AbduSSamad. Some people spell the combination with a front vowel Abdelhadi instead of Abdulhadi or 'Abdulhaadi, and Abdelrahim instead of Abdulrahim or 'AbdurraHiim.
24. In their linguistic structure these names take a combination of two nominals as Abdu+Allah, Abuu+ Bakar or a nominal + a definite article al+another nominal, as in Abdu-al+Jabbaar,

Jamaal+al+Diin, and Wariithu+al+Diin. Some people write this compounded name as two separate words but some combine the two. A good example is 'Abd Allah and Abdallah. Some names are formed from a combination of two names as in MuHammed-SaalaH (MuHammad the good), MuHammed-al-Maahiri (MuHammad the smart), MuHammed-Saadiq (MuHammad the trustworthy), Siraaju-lmulk (the light of kings), Mu'izz-al-Dawla (the glorifier of the state).

25. The name MuSTafaa is derived from S-f-w 'chose' and is of verb form VIII, ifti'aal. The name becomes IStafwa and then IStafaa. The t which appears next to the velarized consonant S is then influenced by it and changes to T becoming ISTafaa 'one chose.' This verb then is changed to a noun and becomes the name MuSTafaa 'the chosen one.' MuStafaa may also be used for other prophets.

26. He is the fourth Khalifa, vicegerent, the first Imam of the Shi'a sect of Islam and cousin of the Prophet.

27. See *Nahjul Balagha Peak of Eloquence, Sermons, Letters and Sayings of Imam Ali ibn Abu Talibn*, Tahrike Tarsile Qur'an, Inc., New York,1982. p.430.

28. Prophet MuHammad married Khadija his first wife when he was twenty-five years old and she was forty. He did not marry again until after her death. The other ten women with whom he consummated marriage had all but one, that is 'Aisha, been married before and were not chosen because of their looks or wealth but for a social reason of establishing links and harmonious relationships with the other tribes and in order to help those women who had lost their husbands.

29. Safiyya means 'the chosen one' from the root S-f-w. She was a Jewish woman who became Prophet MuHammad's seventh wife. She died in A.D.672.

30. Sura 108.

31. Sura 20 verse 1.

32. Yaasiin, Surah 26 verse 1.

33. It is a title for Sura 73.

34. See Sura 3 verse 160.

35. There are two months called by this name, Rabii' al-awwal, the first Rabii', and Rabii' al-thaanii, the second Rabii'. Rabii' also means spring.

36. Mwana Idi is Swahili for a girl. Dhulhijjah the eleventh month

and one of pilgrimage to Mecca to perform hajj provides names Haji and Hija for boys and girls.

37. The statement about this journey appears in Sura 17 verse 1.

CHAPTER FOUR

ARABIC MUSLIM NAMES

The Arabic language provides a rich source of names for Muslims. Phenomena ranging from natural geophysical elements, astronomy, the weather, the animal kingdom, abstract ideas that represent different desirable concepts, and events that take place in the lives of one's parents give rise to personal names.

To give some examples of boys' names

1. From Nature

Akhtar	constellation
Badru	full moon
Bahraam	Mars
Hilaal	crescent
Kawkab	star
Mmah and Mmaaha	crystal, moon
Naajum	star
Nasiim	breeze
Qamar and Qamariyyah	full moon
Rabaab	white clouds
Shamsu	sun
Shihaab	shooting star

Sitaar	star, shield
Suhayl	constellation, Sirius
Surya	sun
Taariq	star
Talaal	clouds
Thary/ Thurayy	Pleiades
Zaahor/Zuhra	Venus
Zuhr/Zuhayr	Venus

Examples of girls' names include:

'Anaan	clouds
Anwar	rays of light
Areej	pleasant breeze
Badriyyah/Badr	full moon
Bahiirah	dazzling
Barjiis/Bargiis	Jupiter
Falak	astronomy
Ghusaama	black cloud
Makiin	calm, serene
Manaar	lighthouse, guiding light
Mmah/Mmaaha	crystal, moon
Muzayna	white cloud
Najma/Nujuum	star
Nasiim	breeze
Nuuriyya	luminous
Ramla	divination, predictor of the future
Saariyah	night clouds
Shamsiyya	sun
SiHaaba	white cloud
Staara	star, shield
Suhayla	Sirius, brightest star, Dog Star
Suraya	sun
Thurayya	Pleiades
Zuhra	Venus

2) From Plants and Perfumery
   Names for girls include:

'Anbar/'Ambar	tree which produces resin
Azhaar	flowers
Daaliya	flower, espalier for grapevines
GhuSuun/GhuSun	branches
Kaamilyaa	beautiful flower, perfection
Kheyzraan/a	bamboo (mother of Haruun Al-Rashiid)
Lawz	almond
Lubnaa	storax tree
Luuqa	fresh dates
Misk	musk
Nargis/Narjis	narcissus
Nawwaar	white flower, blossom
Nu'maan	a red plant
Rehaan/Rehaana	basel, beautiful scent
Rummaana	pomegranate
Sabr/Sabra	aloe, endurance, patience
Sawsaan	type of tree
Sha'ba	branch
Shajara	tree
Shajar-ad-durr	tree of pearls, plant
Shamiim	beautiful scent
Shayba	artemisia
Thamra/Thamara	bearing fruit, productive
TuffaaHa	apple
Tuut	mulberry
Warda	rose
Wardulmunaa	rose of happiness
Yasmiin	jasmin
Za'faraan	saffron
Zabiib/Zabeeb	raisins

Zahra	flower, blossom
Zaytuun	olive, guava
Zuhuur/Zuhuura	flowers

Examples of boys' names include:

Abuu-Zaydaan	a medicinal plant
'Anbar	ambergris
Faakih	fruit, good-natured
GhuSuun	branches
Kattaani	linen
Khayzaraan	bamboo
KhiDr	greenery, greengrocer
Khuzaamaa	lavender
Kimaama	sheath of date palm
Lawz	almond
Liina	date palm
Luuqa	fresh dates
Nisriin	white flowers, rose
Nu'maan	a red plant
Rehaan	basel, beautiful scent
Shajara	tree
Shayba	artemisia
Tamr	date
Thaamir	producing fruits, productive
Zabiib/Zabeeb	raisins

3) From Animals

The animal kingdom also contributes its share of desired qualities of beauty and bravery. These include the following names for boys:

'Abbaas	lion, stern
'Andaliib	nightingale, beautiful voice
'Antar/'Antara	blue flies, brave, hero
Asad	lion, strong

'Azzaam	lion, srong
Baazii	hawk, sharp
Bakr	young camel, reliable
Dhi'b	wolf, swiftness
Dhiyaab	wolves
Dhu'ayyib	young wolf
Faaris	horseman, knight, hero
Fahad/Fehed	panther, powerful
FaHal	bull, outstanding
Faniiq	beautiful stallion, swift
FiTaam	young falcon, sharp
Ghazaal/Ghazaala	antelope, handsome
Ghazaali	antelope, handsome[1]
Ghuul	demon, snake
Hadal	dove
HafS	cub, strength
Hamaam	pigeon, messenger
Hamza	lion, strong
Hassuun	goldfinch, beauty
Hawaam	lion, strength
Haydar	lion, strength
HaySam	lion, strength, power
Haytham	young eagle, sharp
Hind	hundreds of camels, wealth
Hurayra	kitten, ill-tempered
Kulayb	small dog, young animal
Kulthuum	elephant, fat face
Na'aama	ostrich, beauty
Numayr	young leopard, strength
Nusayr	young eagle, sharp
QiTTa	cat
Samak	fish
Saqr	small falcon, sharp
Shaahiin	falcon, insight
Shaatuu	young goat, kid

Shabath	spider, protective
ShabuuT	fish
Shibli	lion cub
SirHaan/SarHaan	wolf, sharp, swift
Subay'	cub, swift
Tha'lab	fox, swift
Usaama	lion, strong
'USfuur	sparrow
'Uthmaan	young reptile, snake
Yamaam	wild pigeon

Examples of girls' names are far fewer but include:

Arwaa	female mountain goat
Asada	lioness, strong
'Azzah	young female gazelle, beauty
BaTTa	duck
Duraa	female parrot, talkative
Faakhita	wild pigeon
Faniiq	beautiful stallion
Fazzaara	female leopard, strength
Ghazaala	antelope, beauty
HafSa	cub, young lioness
Hamaama	pigeon
Haydara	lioness, strength
Hind	hundreds of camels, wealth
Hurayra	small cat, ill-tempered
Khawla/Khola	female gazelle, beauty
Labwa	lioness
Maariyya	calf
Mahaa	wild cow
Mayya	monkey
Na'aama	bird
NaHla	bee
Rashaa	young gazelle

Reem/Riima	white gazelle, beauty
Salwa	quail
Shahiin	falcon, insight
Taawuus	peacock, beauty
Tha'laba	fox, swift
Tuwayra	little bird
Zabiyya	female gazelle

4) From Land, Gem Stones and Precious Metals
Some girls are compared to precious stones or metals:

Almaas	diamond
BaTTa	duck
Buthayna	soft ground
Daana	pearl
Dhahab	gold
Fairuuz/Feruuz	turquoise
FiDDa	silver
Hajar	stones
Jawhar/Johar/Jawhara	jewel
Lulu	pearl
Marjaan	red coral
NuDaar	gold
Nuura	shining stone
Sawda	land which is black
Ya'aquut	sapphire
Yamaama	wild pigeon
Zumarrad	emerald

These names which are also used for boys include:

Almaas	diamond
Dhahab	gold
Fairuuz/Feruuz	turquoise
Hazn	hard ground

Hudhaym	a sharp sword
Jawhar/Johar	jewel
Marjaan	red coral
Safwaan	stony land
Ya'aquut	sapphire
Zumarrad	emerald

5) From Water for boys:

BaHar	ocean
Bilaal	dampness of rain
Ja'far	small river
Nahar	river

for girls:

| Maawiya | water |

6) From Colors for boys:

AbyaD	white
Ad-ham	black
AHmar	red
AkhDar	green
Aswad	black
Azraq	blue
Juwayn	dim. of black
KhiDr	green
Kulf	brownish
Maazin	light, white
Mash'al	light color, flame
Sahiib	reddish brown
Samar	dark, brown
SuHaym	young black
Suwayd/Suwed	dim. of black

for girls:

Admaa'	brown
Arjuwaan	red
Dujjy	darkness of the night
KhaDra	green
Kulfa	brownish
Mashaa'il	light
Samra	brown
Sawdaa'	black

7) From Occupations and Titles

Occupations and titles provide another source of personal names for boys:

Abuuruus	father of chiefs
Akkaar	laborer
Amiir	prince
'ATTaar	perfumer
Baab/ baaba	father
BaHHaar	sailor
Bannaa	mason, builder
Baqriy	cattle merchant
Darwesh	religious, pious
FallaaH	farmer
Fannaan	artist
Farraar	refugee
Fataa/Faati	youth, brave
FaTiin	expert
Fattaash	researcher, explorer
Ghariib	foreigner, traveller
Haakim	judge
Haaris	watchman, protector
Haarith	plowman, tiller
Haarub	fighter, warrior

Haddaad	ironsmith
Hajj	one who has been on a pilgrimage
'Ibaada	worshipper
Imaam	leader
Jazzaar	butcher
Jinddi/Ginddii	soldier
Kamiish	skilful
Kattaany	works with linen
Khaan	leader
Khaliifa	viceregent, successor
KhaTiib	orator
Lodhi/Luudhi	looks for shelter
Luqmaan	the wise one
Maalik/Maliik	king
ManSab	dignified
Maulana	our master
Mu'allim	teacher
Mufti	legal adviser
Munajjim	astrologer
NaHHaas	coppersmith
Najjaami	astrologer
Najjaar	carpenter
Naqqaash	sculptor, painter
QaaDi	judge
Qarjii/Garjii	wholesaler
QaSSaab	butcher
Qaysar	emperor
Raawiyah	narrator
Raaza	mason
Rais	head, leader
Sayyid	chief, master
Shah	king, emperor
Shariif	descendant of Prophet MuHammad, honorable

Sheikh	leader, elderly
SulTaan	ruler
Taalib	student
Ustaadh	mister, professor
Wakiil	representative, attorney
Walii	governor
Waziir	minister

Those names which have female equivalents include:

Amiira	princess
Bibi	lady
Diina	religious girl
FaTiin	expert
Haarub/Harbiyya	fighter
Hadaada	ironsmith
Hajja/Hajjiyya	one who has been on a pilgrimage
Hakiima	judge
Hartha	plowwoman, tiller
KhaTiiba	orator
Maliika	queen
Mu'allima	teacher
Munajjima	astrologer
QaaDiya	judge
Raisa	leader
Sayyida	lady
Sharifa	descendant of Prophet Muhammad
MuHammad	honorable
Sheikha	leader
SulTaana	ruler
Taaliba	student
Ustaadha	professor

Changes have occurred over time in the form, meaning and significance of some of the names. Underlying concepts that we see today as secular once had religious significance in pre-Islamic times. The sun and moon provide deep forests of meaning when they provide inspiration for personal names. The ancient Sabian Arabs of south-western Arabia once worshipped the moon and the sun as deities, the Sun Goddess and the Moon God. The idea of a Moon God may be traced back to the ancient Egyptians. We do not know the origin of the Sun Goddess. In Arabic the noun *qamar*, moon, is of masculine gender and the noun *shams*, sun, is feminine.

NOTES

1. Notice the difference in pronunciation between Al-Ghazaalii and Al-Ghazzaalii; the second name is derived from ghazzal meaning a spinner.

CHAPTER FIVE

ROOTS AND DERIVATIONS

The study of names, onomatology, is a science. Some readers may be interested in the linguistic aspect of names and this is a chapter for them. We shall examine the structure of Muslim names, their roots and derivations, their grammatical categories, their spellings and their adaptation to the Hausa-Fulani and the Swahili languages.

BASIC ROOT AND VOWEL PATTERNS

The Arabic language generates many new and fresh names for young parents searching for uniqueness because the very structure of the language allows a proliferation of names.

All names, old and new, are derived from a basic consonantal root that has a basic meaning. It is then combined with various vowel patterns to produce different forms of words and thus different names. To illustrate this I shall discuss five roots with their derivations. All five are very productive. At least ten names can be formed from each, yet the basic meaning always remains the same.

The first group of names is based on the notion of praise, the second on goodness, the third on safety, the fourth on happiness and the fifth on gratitude. What changes from one name to the other is the linguistic form, the message and the bearer of the name.

1. The root H-m-d which gives the verb hamida 'he praised' generates the following names:

Hamd (praise), Hamda (f. praise), Hamydy (grateful), Hamdiyya (f.), Haamid, Hamiid (praiseworthy), Hamiida (praiseworthy), Hamuud (praised), Hammaad (praises), Hamaada (praise), Humuud (praiseworthy), Humayd (dim. of Humuud), Humayda (f.) AHmad/AHmed (more commendable), MuHammad (praised), MaHmuud (commendable, praised), Haamid (one who praises), Hamuude (praiseworthy female), Hamed (praised), Hammudah (commendable), Hamdaan (double praise), Hammaad (praiser), Hamiidaan (who praise), Hamduun (dim.) and MuHaymid (praises).

2. The root H-s-n which gives the verb hasuna 'he did well' generates:

Hasan (good, handsome), Husayn or Hussain (dim. of Hasan), Hasnaa' (beautiful woman), MaHsin, MuHsin (beneficent), MuHsina (beneficent woman), Hasiina (beautiful woman), Husnaa (beautiful), Hassaan (good one), Hasnuu (good), Husnaa (amicable), Husni (the best), Husniyya (the best), Hasanayn (very good), Hassuun (who does good), Haasin (the good one, the moon) Hasanaat (good deeds), MaHaasin (good treatment), Husn (handsome), Husna (beautiful), TaHsiin (embellishment), IHsaan (beneficence).

3. The root s-l-m which gives the verb salima 'he was safe' generates:

Saalim (he is safe, secure), Saliim (safe), Saalum, Salaama (soundness, peaceful), Salmaan (secure), Salmiin (secure), Suluuma,(peaceful, Muslim), Muslima (Muslim woman), Aslam (safer), Islam (submission, Islam), Sulmaa (peacefulness), Salaam (peaceful male), Salamuu (peaceful f.), Selma (peace), Sulaym (safe, dim. of Sulm/Sulmaa/ Saliim/Sulamaa) Sulaymaan/Slemaan (safe, double of

Sulayma), Musallam/Msellem (flawless).

4. The root s-'-d gives the verb sa'ada 'he helped,' i.e. he made one happy, generates:

Sa'd (good luck), Su'uud (pl. of sa'd), Sa'iid/Sa'eed and Sa'iida (happy, lucky), Su'aad (happiness), Mus'ad (fortunate), Mas'uud and Mas'uuda (happy), As'ad (happier), Sa'di (happy), Sa'iida (happy), Sa'diyya (fortunate, happy) Mas'ad (support), Su'uuda or Sa'aada (happiness).

5. The root sh-k-r which gives the verb shakara 'he thanked' generates: Shukuur (thankfulness), Shukrii (thanks, thanking),

Shakuur (thankful), Shaakir (grateful), Shakiir (thankful), Shukriyya (thanking f.), Shukraan (gratitude m. and f.), Shukuur (thankfulness, pl.).

NOUNS AND VERBS

Most people's names are nouns that have other references and are derived from basic verbal roots. A few have been fashioned from verbs. Examples include:

Haajar	he emigrated, abandoned
Hadaa	he was tranquil
Hamad	he praised
Yahya	he lives
Ya'iish	he lives
Ya'quub	he follows
Yaziid	he increases

All these names have been in use for a long time but new names have also appeared. One recent example I have heard is

Yaf'al	he acts

This may be derived from the verse in the Qur'aan which reads:

Inna Llaha yaf'alu maa yuriid[1]
God does what He wishes.

These names refer to a masculine singular third person. The first three: *Haajar*, *Hadaa* and *Hamada* are in the perfect (past) tense. The last four with the ya- prefix indicate present tense. Most of the rest of the names are technically verb-noun or noun in their morphological structure.

GENDER - MASCULINE AND FEMININE

Many Arabic Muslim names are of a descriptive nature derived from everyday language and therefore are used by Muslims and non-Muslims. These pertain to a person's own character or his or her relation to others. Gender distinctions therefore become linguistically, socially and culturally relevant and necessary in the formation of a name. Personal names thus have masculine and feminine forms. They include:

Masculine	Feminine	Meaning
'Aabid	'Aabida	worshipper
'Aadil	'Aadila	just
'Aa'id	'Aaida	recurrent, gain
'Aalii	'Aaliya	exalted
'Aalim	'Aalima	learned
'Aamir	'Aamira	prosperous
'Aaqil	'Aaqila	sensible
'Aarif	'Aarifa	knowledgeable
'AaSim	'AaSima	protected
Aasiy	Aasiya	a good person
'AaTif	'AaTifa	kind
'Aatik	'Aatika	sincere
Adiib	Adiiba	well mannered

'Adil	'Adila	just,fair
'Aish	'Aisha	alive/life
Amaan	Amaana	trust
Amiin	Amiina/Ammuun	trustworthy
'Aqiil	'Aqiila	wise
ASiil	ASsiila	of good lineage
'Aziiz	'Aziiza	precious
Badr	Badriyya	full moon
Bahii/Bahaa	Bahiyya	bright
Basiir	BaSiira	perceptive
Bashshaar	Bashshaara	messenger of good news

Bassaam/Baasim	Basma	smile
Daliil	Daliila	guide
Dhahab/Dhahabii	Dhahabiyya	golden
Faadii	Faadiya	redeemer
FaaDil	FaDiil/ FaDiila	victorious
Fahiim	Fahiima	learned
Faiq	Faaiqa	superb
Faiz	Faaiza	successful
Fakhri	Fakhriyya	pride
Fannaan	Fannaana	artist
FaraH	FarHa	happiness
FarHaan	FarHaana	happy
FarHi	FarHiya	joyful
Fariid	Fariida	unique
Farraar	Farraara	refugee
FaTiin	FaTiina	intelligent
Fauzi	Fauziyya	successful
Ghanii	Ghaniyya	wealthy

Haady	Hadiyya	guide
HaafiZ	HafiiZa	preserver
Haamid	Haamida	grateful
Haashim	Hashiima	respectful
Habaab	Habaaba	loved
Habiib	Habiiba	beloved
HafiiZ	HafiiZa	preserver
Hakiim	Hakiima	wise
Haliim	Haliima	gentle
Hamd	Hamda	praise
Hamd	Hamda	gratitude
Hamduun	Hamduuna	praise (dim.)
Hamdy	Hamdiyya	grateful
Hamiid	Hamiida	grateful
Haniif	Haniifa	true believer
Hasan	Hasna/Hasiina	good
Hasiib	Hasiiba	noble
Hassaan	Hassaana	adored
Hijmaan	Hijmaana	strong
Hilaal	Hilaala	crescent
Jaabir	Jaabira	brave
Jaadhib	Jaadhiba/	
	Jadhbiyya	beauty
Jaasir	Jaasira	courageous
Jaliil	Jaliila	celebrity
Jamiil	Jamiila	beautiful
Jawhar	Jawhara	gem
Kaamil/Kamiil	Kaamila/Kamiila	perfection
KaaZim	KaaZima	restrained
Kariim	Kariima	generous
Khaalid	Khaalida	friend
Khaatim	Khaatima	last
Khabiir	Khabiira	cognizant
KhiDr	KhaDraa'/	
	KhaDra	green, fertility

Labiib	Labiiba	lovable
LaTiif	LaTiifa	gentle
Maahir	Maahira	expert
Maajid	Maajida	diligent
Maati'	Maati'a	outstanding
MaHbuub	NMaHbuuba	beloved
MaHfuuZ	MaHfuuZa	protected
Maliik/Maalik	Maliika	ruler
MaliiH	MaliiHa	handsome
Makky	Makkiyya	Mecca
Mastuur	Mastuura	covered
Ma'Suum	Ma'Suuma	perfect
Mayaas	Mayaasa	proud, dignified
Maymuun	Maymuuna	blessed
Mudrik	Mudrika	reasonable
Mufiid	Mufiida	useful
Muniir	Muniira	bright
Muslim	Muslima	Muslim
Naail	Naaila	achiever
Naayif	Naayifa	upright
Nabiil	Nabiila	noble
Nadhiir	Nadhiira	consecrated to God
Nafiis	Nafiisa	valuable
Na'iim	Na'iima	comfortable
NaSiib	NaSiiba	lucky
NuuH	NuuHa	sway, howl
RaabiH	RaabiHa	gain
RaaDi	RaDiyya	contented
RaaDii	RaDiyya	satisfied
Raaghib	Raaghiba	ambition, desire
Raajii	Raajiya	hope
Raatib	Raatiba	organizer
Raawii	Raawiya	entertainer
Rafii'	Rafii'a	exalted

69

RaHiil	RaHiila	traveller
RaHiim	RaHiima	compassionate
Rashiid	Rashiida	sensible
Ratiib	Ratiiba	monotonous
RayHaan	RayHaana	beautiful scent
ReHaan	Rehaana	sweet smell, basil
Saabir	Saabira	patient
Sa'ad	Sa'da	happy
Saafi	Saafiya	pure, sincere
SaaHib	SaaHiba	companion
SaalaH	SalHa	goodness
SaaliH	SaaliHa	goodness
Saalim	Salma	safe
Saami	Saamiya	exalted
Sabbuur	Sabuura	patient
SabiiH	SabiiHa	good looking
Sa'd	Sa'da	happiness
Sadiiq	Sadiiqa	trustworthy
Saghiir	Saghiira	small
Sa'iid	Sa'iida	happy
Sakhiy	Sakhiyya	generous
Salaam	Salaama	peace
Saliim	Saliima	safe
Salm	Salma	secure
SamiiH	SamiiHa	forgiver
Samiir/Sameer	Samiira	companion
Sha'bii	Sha'biyya	branches out
Shaadii	Shaadiya	singer, exert
Shaafi	Shaafiya	healer
Shabiib	Shabiiba	youthfulness
Shafiiq	Shafiiqa	compassionate
Shahiid	Shahiida	martyr, witness
Shahiir	Shahiira	famous
Shariif	Shariifa	noble
Sheikh	Sheikha	leader

SiHaab	SiHaaba	cloudy, generous
Subhi	SubHiyya	beautiful
Suhayl	Suhayla	star
SulTaan	SulTaana	ruler
Taahir	Taahira	clean
Taalib	Taaliba	student
Tamiim	Tamiima	perfect
Tawfiiq	Tawfiiqa	success
Tayyib	Tayyiba	good
Thaabit	Thaabita	firm
Thamiin	Thamiina	valuable
Wahab	Wahba	gift
WaHiid	WaHiida	unique
Wajiih	Wajiha	distinguished
Zaahir	Zaahira	beautiful
Zaki/Zaakii	Zakiyya	virtuous
Zakii	Zakiyya	excellence
Zeen	Zeena	beautiful
Ziin/Zeen	Zena/Ziina	beautiful

It will be seen that in the names listed above the first form of each pair is masculine and the second has the feminine suffix a/-ah added to it. Some masculine names may be given a feminine suffix. The grammatical function of this suffix is to indicate a singular noun of a group of items or mass noun. For example

| TawHiid | TawHiida | unity of God |
| Tawiil | Tawiila | tall |

shajar means trees *shajara* is a tree. The suffix that is added is known as t marbuuTa in Arabic. This means a closed t which is dropped when one pauses. Masculine names which appear with this ending include:

'atiyyah	gift
Barakah	blessing
Burdah	garment
Dalaamah	tall
Haaritha	tiller
HafiiZa	attentive
Hamaada	praise
Hamiida	praiseworthy
Hamza	in control
Hartha	tiller
Hassuuna	goldfinch
Hibba	gift
Hidaaya	gift
Hurayra	young cat
'Ibaada	worshipping
Khaliifa	successor
Khamiisa	born on Thursday
Kinaana	quiver, tribe
Maysara	easiness, comfort
Mu'aawiya	name of a tribe
Mughiira	deep in knowledge

Na'ma	prosperity
Nu'ayma	happiness, blessing
Nuwayra	small fire
Nuzha	honesty
Rabii'a	iron helmet, strong
RawaaHa	return
Rufaa'a	dignity
SabiiHa	morning
Salma	peaceful
Sawaada	great number, master, blackness
Sha'ba	branches out
Shabaaba	youth
ShaHama	grease, fat
Shajara	tree
Sulma	peace
TalHa	name of a place, acacia tree
Tharwa/Tharwat	wealth
'Ubayda	young worshipper
'Umaara	structure, squadron
Umayya	a tribe of Quraish
'Uqba	stage of a journey, remainder
'Urwa	bond of friendship
Usaama	lion
'Utba	proof
Wadii'a	quiet, peaceful
Zaaida	increase
Zam'a	determination
Zur'a	cultivation
Zuraara	missile, button

Most of the above names do not distinguish gender in usage. Those which are used only for boys are *Hamza, Kinaana, Khalifa, Mu'awiya,'Ubayda, 'Umaara, Umayya, 'Uqba* and *Usaama*. Other Muslim names that do not distinguish gender and may be given to either boys or girls include:

Aalaa'	blessings
Aathaar	sign
Ahdaaf	goal, great
AHsan	lovelier
Almaas	diamond
Aluuf	adorable
Amaan	security
Amaani	trustworthy
Amjaad	dignity
Anas	entertain
Anuus	jolly
Anwaar	light
Arab	need
'Ariif	cognizant
Ariij	beautiful smell
Ashraf	more honorable
AshTar	smarter
ASlii	original
Athaar	footstep, tradition
Athiil	noble
Ayman	blessed
Azaal	eternity
Azur	strength

BajjaH	cheerful
Bishaara	good news
GhuSuun	branches
Hadaa	tranquil
Haniin	longing
Hannaan	affectionate
Hayaat	life
Hind	a large flock of camels, wealth
Ibtihaaj	happiness
Ibtihaal	prayer
Ibtisaam	a smile
Idraak	achiever
Iftikaar	intellectual
Iftikhaar	dignified
IHsaan	beneficence
IHtiraam	respect
IkhlaaS	devotion, sincere
Ilhaam	inspiration
Imtiyaaz	distinguished
Inshiraah	happy
Intisaar	victory
Iqbaal	arrival, thriving
Is'aad	bliss
Isaaf	land
Is'aaf	help
Ishraaf	control
Ishraaq	radiance
ISlaah	reconciliation
'ISmat/'ISma	rope to hold to
Ithaar	preference, affection
I'tidaal	compromise, moderate
I'timaad	reliable, dependable
Iymaan	faith, compassion
Jihaad	exert effort
Kawkab	star

Khuzayma/Khuzma	lavender
Mahaasin	good work
MaHjuub/MaHjoub	veiled, hidden
Majd	diligent
Nahaar	daytime
NajaaH	success
Nasiim	breeze
Nawf	eminent
Nuur	light
RabaaH	gain
Rabwa	height
Rubeyya	nourishment
Sabriyn/Saabriyn	are patient
Safaa'	serenity, clearness
Salmaa	safe
Sharaafddin	the honor of the religion
Waddi	affectionate
Wafaa'	accomplishment
Wisaam	beautiful mark
Zaytuun	olive, guava
Ziin/Zeen	beautiful, good looking
Zubaida	a piece of butter

This list thus provides names for those who may prefer a genderless name for their newborn.

COMPARATIVE FORM

Names such as *Akbar* 'the greatest' are in a comparative/superlative form. Other boys' names of this type include:

AfDal	better, best
AfraH	happier, happiest
AHmad	more, most grateful
AHsan	better, best

AkhTar	more, most equal
Akram	more, most generous
Anwar	brighter, brightest
Ariib	more, most intelligent
Arshad	more, most sensible
As'ad	happier, happiest
ASghar	smaller, smallest
Ash'ab	more miserly (legendary figure)
Ash'ar	distinctive, cares
Ashja'	braver, bravest
Ashqar	fair complexion
Ashraf	nobler, noblest
Ashraq	shine
AshTar	smarter, smartest
Aslam	safer, safest
Asmar	browner, brownest
Aswad	more black, master
Ayman	happiness

The feminine forms of these names take a morphological form of fu'laa (CVCCVV)in Arabic as in:

Sa'daa'
Salwaa
Samraa
Sawdaa'
Sughraa

Some names have a diminutive form. It is given to a grand-daughter when she is her grandmother's namesake to avoid mentioning the grandmother's name, or is adopted for the second child when the parents wish to bestow the same conceptual idea on their second child as on their first. This is believed to give the two children a specially close relationship. The most famous such pair is Hasan and Husayn, the grandchildren of Prophet MuHammad and this pairing is popularly adopted by Muslim parents worldwide.

Other diminutive forms include the name of the famous king and Prophet *Sulaymaan* [derived from S-l-m which became *Sulam* with a diminutive *Sulaym* and then acquired a dual suffix -aan producing *Sulaymaan*].

Other examples of diminutive nouns are:

Regular	Diminutive	Meaning
'Abd	'Ubayd	worshipper
'Adhba	'Udhayba	pleasant
Asad	Usayd	young lion
Aswad	Suwayd	black, greater
Azraq	Zurayq	blue
BaHar	BuHayr	sea
Bakht	Bukhayt	luck
Bishaar	Bashiyr	messenger of good news
Buthna	Buthaynaa	piece of land
FarH	FariyH	joy
Hamed	Humayd	praise
Hind	Hunayd	flock of camels, wealth
Humuud	Humayyid	grateful
Jabr	Jubayr	powerful
Jawn	Juwayn	black
Khaalid	Khuwaylid	glorious, lasting
NaSiib	NuSayb	luck
Riim	Ruwaym	white gazelle
Sab'	Subay'	young lion
Sakiina	Sukayna	calmness
Salluum	Sulaym	peaceful
Salma	Sulayma	peaceful
Sayf	Suwayf	small sword
Sha'b	Shu'ayb	popular, branches out

Suud	Suwayd	master, black
Ṭifl	Ṭufayl	delicate
'Umar	'Umayr	lifetime
Umm	Umayma	mother
Ummat	Umayya	tribe
Zubda	Zubayda	butter, delicate
Zuhur	Zuhayr	bright, blooming

Another pattern of diminutive nouns consists of names such as:

Faiza	Faizuun	success
Hamad	Hammuud	gracious
Hamd	Hamduun	praise
Khaalid	Khalduun	lasting
Sa'd	Su'uud	happiness
Zayd	Zayduun	increase

A possible second name may be formed from a dual suffix -ayn/-eyn that may be added to a regular name. This reinforces the meaning of the name and provides the second of the pair as in:

Hasan 'good' and Hasaneyn 'doubly good'
Sulaym 'peaceful' and Sulaymaan 'doubly peaceful'

Other examples include boys' names such as:

'Adnaan
'Affaan
'Azzaan
Hamdaan
'Imraan
'Irfaan
Jabraan/Jubraan
Jum'aan

79

Nabhaan
Nu'maan
RamaDaan
RayHaan
RiDwaan
Safwaan
Salmaan
Shamlaan
'Uthman

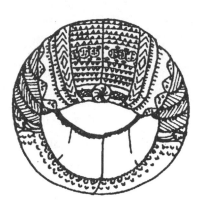

Examples for girls are:

'Irfaan
Meyyaan
Rayhaana

The different categories of names convey morphological forms prevalent in the linguistic structure of the Arabic language and familiar only to those who are familiar with the language.

NAMES AND THEIR SPELLING

The problem confronting many users of African Muslim names writing in Roman script is how to spell their names to convey their correct pronunciation and meaning. Certain consonants that do not exist in African languages such as the emphatic letters are dropped or replaced.[2] Vowels are added to break clusters that are not common in Hausa or in Kiswahili, and length of both consonants and vowels is sometimes ignored. These phonological changes are magnified because of the multiple derivations possible from one basic root.

In order for the meaning of a name to be intelligible without any ambiguity it must be correctly spelt. The presentation of some of the names in English script results unfortunately in ambiguity.

Take, for instance, the name that is spelt Tarik in

English. Is this name derived from Taarik (he relinquishes) or Ṯaariq (he strikes, star) or Ṯariiq (road). Its meaning and pronunciation are not clear.

Similarly, the name Asad (lion) is pronounced differently from As'ad (happier, happiest) but when both are written Asad in English there is no way of knowing which of the two meanings applies.

The name spelt Hajar similarly conveys two different meanings. When pronounced with the English h as in 'had,' it means 'to emigrate,' but with the sound H in Arabic Hajar it means 'stones.' The way a word is spelt invites different pronunciations. To those who are not familiar with the intended form this does not matter, but for those who know the language, each way of pronouncing the name generates a different meaning. Most people are concerned that their names should not be misspelt or mispronounced.[3] They find this inaccurate and irritating.

I would here refer the reader to my previous discussion of the names Malik (monarch), Maliik (king, owner) and Maalik (ruler, owner). All are derived from the same root m-l-k (to own) and mean more or less the same, as you can see, but when the name is spelt in English Malik it is difficult to know how to refer to the right form and its pronunciation. Similarly Salim stands for Saalim (safe, secure) and Saliim (safe, secure), a change in pronunciation caused by the syllable one stresses or vowel lengthening. In order to identify the right person one needs to hear the name[4] and to spell it correctly to be familiar with the way a person prefers to spell his name. He will learn whether it is MaHmuud, Mahmoud, Mahmood, MaHmuud or Mahmud. People are usually unhappy when their names are misspelt or mispronounced.

History is also misinterpreted when names do not convey explicitly their personalities or individuals. I mentioned in my last book the difficulty of recognizing from the Latinized versions of Alpharabius, Avicenna, Averroes and Avempace, the Muslim scientists and philosophers, MuHammad ibn-MuHammad ibn Tarkhaan abu-NaSr Al-

Faraabi (A.H. 258-339 or A.D.869-950), Abu-'Ali al-Husayn ibn Siina (A.H. 370-428 or A.D.980-1037), Abu-al-Waliid MuHammad ibn-AHmad ibn Rushd (A.H. 520-595 or A.D.1126-1198) and Abu Bakr MuHammad ibn YaHya ibn BaajjaH (d. A.D.1138). Given Latin names, their scholarly contributions are attributed wrongly to the history of European science and their cultural identities, as Muslims, concealed.

Some variations in the spelling of a name are harmless since they do not cause conceptual ambiguity. For example, whether one spells Adam, Adamou or Adamu, Haruun or Haruna,'Umar, Umar or Omar, Yusuf, Yusufu or Yusufa, Amna or Amne, Fatma or Fatuma, 'Aisha, Esha, Asha or Ayisha, Layla or Lela, Rayya or Reyye, Sharifa, Sharifah, Sherifa or Sharife, Jamiila, Jamilah, Djamilla or Jamile is unimportant. The sets in each case are derived from the same root and the different spellings simply convey dialectal variations, grammatical assimilation, language adaptations or one's transliteration. Nevertheless, a certain way of spelling a name in English may be closer to the original Arabic sounds than others. For instance, the name Muniir may be written in English script Muniyr, Munir, Muneer, Moonir, Munier and Mounir. The last two ways of spelling this name do not convey the pronunciation of the original sound and meaning and should be avoided. The girl's name written in English as Sana conveys neither its correct meaning 'brilliant' nor its pronunciation when it is not written Sanaa'. Many other examples will be seen in the lists of names I present in Part Two.

NOTES

1. Al-Baqra, Sura 2 verse 253 and Al'imraan, Sura 3 verse 53 which ends with yaf'alu maa yashaa.
2. The following phonological changes appear in Hausa:
    Arabic: th dh ' H kh S D Z Hausa: s z ' h k/kh s d/r/l z
3. Misspelt names are corrected. For instance, an article appeared in the *New York Times* listing the winners of the 40 Marshall Scholarships awarded by the British Embassy and misspeling one surname. The *New York Times* on December 19, 1995 made the correction. The scholar, at the Massachussets Institute of Technology, was Ciamac C. Moallemi not McAllemi. This shows the sensitivity and importance of spelling and pronouncing a person's name correctly.
4. See Zawawi, 1993, pp.10-12 for further discussion.

CHAPTER SIX

NAME CHANGES

ADOPTION

People change their names for many reasons, social, political and religious. In the United States, for instance, when a couple adopt a child, they are free to change the child's original name, giving it their own family name if they wish. In Islamic society, those who adopt a child have no right to change the child's family or hereditary name on adoption. There are two reasons for this. The first has to do with lawful marriages within the family. Adopted children are permitted to marry within the family into which they have been adopted. The second protects the adopter's biological children from being deprived of any rightful inheritance. Hence an adopted child continues to bear his biological father's family name. If the biological father is unknown, the child will be given the name *ibn Abdullah*, son of 'the servant, worshipper of God.' Of course, not all *Abdullahs* are adopted children.

MARRIAGE

In the United States and many other western countries women change their names to those of their husbands when they marry. This is not the case everywhere.In Spain and Latin America a person may add the mother's family name to that of their father as did the tennis player Arantxa (personal name) Sanchez (father's family name) Vicario (mother's family name). The father's and the mother's names may be joined together with y 'and' as in Jose Ortega y Gassett, the famous Spanish writer. Jose,Christian name, Ortega, father's name and Gasset, mother's surname before marriage. This is not the case in many Muslim societies. Upon marriage a Muslim woman is not required to change her name to that of her husband, although today some 'modernized' Muslim women choose to do this. Some add their father's family name to their husband's family name, hyphenating the two. In the United States this is a modern feature.

IMMIGRATION

Ethiopian, Yemeni and North African children who migrate with their parents to Israel are required to adopt national Jewish names in their new homeland. Because their original given names have personal and cultural significance for them, the change sometimes causes resentment and unhappiness.

In Islamic society names are bestowed on children within forty days of their birth. The expectation is that they will remain with them for life. This may cause problems for Muslim families residing overseas. Take the real case of one East African family, a man and his wife and their five-year old son who came to live in the United States.

The father's name is *Ahmed*, the son of *Said*, who is the son of *Salim*, i.e. *Ahmed bin Said bin Salim*. At work he is known as *Mr.Salim*, i.e. by his grandfather's name.

His wife is *Fatma*, daughter of *Salim*, the son of *Mahfudh*, i.e. *Fatma bint Salim bin Mahfudh*. She is identified as *Mrs. Mahfudh*. She does not wish to give up her father's name because to give up her father's name would be to forsake her ties to her father and her relationship with him.

Their son's personal name is *Mahir bin Ahmed bin Said bin Salim*. To use three names is quite usual among Muslims.

86

At school he is called *Mahir Said*, i.e. by his grandfather's name since that is the last one to appear on his birth certificate.

We see here the confusion that may arise when only surnames or family names are considered. The three members of the same nuclear family appear to be unrelated individuals with three different surnames: *Ahmed Said Salim, Fatma Salim Mahfudh* and *Mahir Said*. Three different surnames for members of the same family!

Ahmed, particularly, is not happy about this alien naming system because it conceals his connection and denies his personal relationship with his son. Should he change his son's name from that of his grandfather who is *Said* to that of his great grandfather *Salim? Fatma*, his wife also has prob-

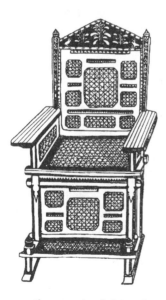

lems with this Americanized naming system. She has a choice of replacing her father's name with that of her husband, or of hyphenating it as *Mahfudh-Salim*, or of keeping her own full maiden name. This is a problem many Muslim women encounter when they are expected to conform to western traditions. The problem predates the feminist movement in the West. This is not a problem back home where in her social interactions she uses both names. *Fatma's* relatives and close friends will refer to her by her father's name as *Fatma Salim* since that is how they have always known her. Her more recently acquired friends and acquaintances will refer to her by her new name, that of her husband, as Mrs. *Salim* or Mme. *Salim* or *Mama Salim* or *Mama Mahir, Mahir's* mother. For those, like *Ahmed* and *Fatma* who live or travel abroad where passport, business and professional contacts with non-Muslims and strangers are required, the problem is a complex one and calls for an appraisal and a solution.

HOW ARE MUSLIM WOMEN SOLVING THIS PROBLEM?

In order to find out, I examined the directory of the Permanent Missions to the United Nations for July 1995. The countries where the Muslim names appeared were Afghanistan, Algeria, Azebaijan, Bahrain, Bangladesh, Burkina Faso, Cameroon, Chad, Djibouti, Egypt, Gambia, Ghana, Guinea, Guinea-Bissau, Iran, Iraq, Jordan, Kuwait, Lebanon, Libya, Malaysia, Mauritania, Morocco, Nigeria, Oman, Pakistan, Saudi Arabia, Senegal, Sudan, Syria, Tajikistan, Tanzannia, Tunisia, Turkey, United Arab Emirates, Uzbekistan and Yemen. I found that the African and non-African Muslim women married to diplomats working at the United Nations take their husbands' names. Women who maintained their own names together with their fathers' came only from Brunei (Darulssalam). Those from Indonesia and Myanmar were divided on the matter. Half of them kept their fathers' names and the other half did not. This suggests that at least for these upper class women there is a tendency upon marriage to take their husbands' names. This is contrary to earlier custom when a woman's name was not affected through marriage. This topic would make an interesting research paper.

Surnames were not used even in the western world before medieval times. For instance, until recently in some places in Europe (e.g.Russia) a person was called by his own name and the father's patronym, irrespective of gender. Hence a woman before marriage was referred to or addressed by her name and her father's name, by her husband's name when she is married, and as a mother of her son when she is a widow.

IDENTIFICATIONS:
CROSSCULTURAL COMBINATIONS

Some people's names burden them with their past as with the European Jewish immigrants who changed their names to Anglo-Saxon sounding ones e.g. Zachariah to Zachary, Shlomo to Solomon, Joseph to Jerry, Jeremiah to Jeremy or Jerry, Rosenbaum to Rowson, Vogel to Bird, Schloss to Castle, Freudmacher to Stanley and Levitch to Lewis, Kahan to Cohen. Some changed the spelling of the name. Others adopted a different name altogether. Their names were sometimes mispronounced and misspelt by an imigration officer.

Others are blessed with reputations that their great-names capture instantly. 'Graf Gives Tour Final a Name It Recognizes' writes a *New York Times* reporter on November 19, 1995.

Professional artists, actors and actresses are free to change their personal names for a better sounding one or to conceal their real identities, as did Judy Garland from Frances Gumm, Susan Hayward from Edythe Marriner, Doris Day from Doris Kappelhoff, Michael Caine from Maurice J. Micklewhite, Fred Astaire from Frederick Austerlitz, Bob Dylan from Robert Zimmerman and Mick Jagger from Michael Philip, to mention but a few. Some writers also choose pseudonyms to conceal their real names: Eric Arthur Blair became George Orwell, Samuel Langhorne Clemens became Mark Twain, Aurore Dudevant became George Sands, Francois Marie Arovet became Voltaire and Carolyn Heilbrun became Amanda Cross. Women assumed male names and men female ones. Most of us stick to our given names, or differently put, our names adhere to us for the rest of our lives. They are a big part of our identity. A recognizable name such as the Kennedy name in the United States may help or hinder a person because it conveys information.

Yet in our contemporary interdependent and changing world, a world of crosscultural contacts, of travelling, intermarriage, conversion, conformity and searching for one's roots, many young people, either from necessity or convenience or simply to be innovative, choose new names for themselves. All capture a contemporary experience: some may reflect so called 'mixed' marriages, some conversions, some political or social perception. These often combine crosscultural elements. Such names have resonance. Hence Martin Bashir a B.B.C. journalist, Rehema Elis N.B.C. reporter, Paula Abdul the American singer, Tarik Winston the dancer, Shaquille O'Neal the basketball player, Karim Abdul Jabbar the football player, Muhammed Ali the boxer, Chris Khan the car salesman, Benjamin Karim the author, Bob Hussain and David Asif American graduate students, Malaika Marie Williams the Rhodes scholar, Kareem Brunner the Harlem store security officer, Lela Rochen the reporter, Safiya Henderson-Holmes the poetess and author, Farid Eastlack the South African nationalist, Nelson Mandela the President of South Africa, all reach out across cultures. Actions, it is sometimes said, speak louder than words. Yet through names we may sometimes discover long lost past actions.

Whenever there is ethnic and religious contact among peoples, intercultural exchanges are sundry and fruitful. Human beings mould culture. Let us take, for example, a truly famous name, that of the first President of India, Jawahar Lal Nehru.

The first name Jawahar in Urdu means a 'jewel.' In Arabic jawahar (the plural noun of the word jawhar) also means a jewel. Lal is Urdu for 'precious stone' from the Arabic la'la' 'to shine or sparkle' (girl would be named *Lulu*, 'a pearl'). Nehru is Urdu for 'canal,' signifying one who lives near a canal. This word is similar to the Arabic noun *nahru* for a river and the verb *nahara* to flow as a stream. A jewel that shines and a flowing river made surely an appropriate name for a leader of Nehru's caliber. Such a name takes on a deeper cultural significance when it is recognized as deriving from the breaking down of language boundaries in the modern world.

Urdu is a lingua franca, like Hausa-Fulani and

Kiswahili, that developed in India as a result of contact between Muslim Arab traders and Hindu inhabitants of India speaking an Indo-Aryan language. As early as the eleventh century a new language and literature had emerged in North India, later expanding to include the eastern and southern parts of the subcontinent. The Urdu language is written in Persian-Arabic script and contains linguistic elements from Arabic, Indian and Farsi (Persian).

CONVERTS TAKING ON NEW NAMES

Since a name is related to identity, converts from one religion to another are changing their identity from what they were to what they wish to be. A change of faith historically and routinely has been accompanied by a change of name. This is so in all religions. There is a conformity between personal names and proclamations of faith.

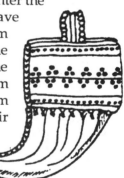

The first group of Muslims to enter the United States after those who might have come with Columbus, were brought from Africa as slaves in the 18th century. Some came directly from Africa, others via the West Indies. Although most came from West Africa, a few were transported from the East African coast. Many lost their names and their Islamic identity.

A second group of Muslims came to the United States from the Middle East in the 19th century. More came later. The third group came from Eastern Europe, India and other parts of the world. According to the 1996 *World Almanac* the Muslim population of the United States is 5,500,000.

A small book *Islam Our Choice* published in Pakistan and distributed by The Young Muslim Association in Nairobi lists forty-eight Americans, Europeans and Japanese who converted to Islam in the 19th and 20th centuries. Among them is a distinguished American diplomat, Muhammad Alexander Russel Webb, who was born in 1846 at Hudson, New York, educated there, and raised as a Presbyterian. He became a journalist and editor of the St. Joseph *Gazette* and of the *Missouri Republican*. In 1887 he was appointed United States Consul at Manila, Philippines. While he was there he studied Islam and changed his name to Muhammad. He died in 1916.[1]

Some converts change their complete name, e.g. Muhammed Ali who was Cassius M. Clay, Kareem Abdul Jabbar from Ferdinand Lewis Alcindor, Imamu Amiri Baraka from Le Roi Jones, Jamil Al-Amin from H.Rap Brown, Ahmed Rashad from Bob Moore, Yusuf Islam from Cat Stevens and Maryam Jameelah from Margaret Marcus. Others adopt a Muslim personal name while retaining in their surname their family connection.

It is not always easy for a convert to Islam to change his name. The American writer Myron Maxwell describes his 'journey' to Islam and the difficulty he had in changing his name to Abdul-Rasheed Muhammad. He writes:

> Suprisingly, unlike many other decisions, choosing Islam was not so difficult. The difficult part, however, was adopting my Muslim name. I believed doing so personally necessary. I felt this would ultimately enhance my Islamic identity, and allow the practice of Islam to be more complete.[2]

Maxwell became Abdul-Rasheed and a Muslim in 1973. Five years later he married Saleemah R. Abdullah who had been born into a Christian (Lutheran) family but had changed her name some time before.

Above are examples of individual converts taking new names. Among the early leaders of Islamic movements in the United States was Timothy Drew born in North Carolina in 1886 who moved later to Newark, New Jersey and became Noble Drew Ali, the leader and founder of a Muslim nationalist movement in 1913. He died in 1929.

Shariff Drew Ali called his organization 'The Moorish Science.' His goal was to liberate non-Caucasian people from western attitudes by changing their psychological outlook and their culture as well as providing them with a world view. He did this by honoring Asian-African history, education and culture. His followers pledged their allegiance to both the United States and to their organization. Their flag was red with a green five-pointed star to symbolize truth, love, peace, justice and freedom. Drew Ali's cultural strategy was the honoring of one's name. His followers were directed to add the word El (the) or Bey (prince, master) to their names to signify their freedom and their world citizenship.

The idea of raising an individual from being a nobody to somebody through a name was pursued further by Elijah Muhammad, the leader in the United States of the Nation of Islam.[3] To their first name his followers appended the letter X in place of their 'slave' names - to liberate them from their 'slave' mentalities. If there are two people in a temple with the same first name, a number is added to the X, e.g Malcolm X 1 and Malcom X 2 to differentiate between them. The change of name removed his Nation of Islam followers from their symbolic slave status. The X then symbolized their unknown African identity.

Malcolm X. was an early follower of Elijah Muhammad. He changed his name three times during his life time, each name representing progressive changes in his religious and political ideology. Born in 1925, he first changed his baptismal name of Malcolm Little to Malcolm X when he joined the Nation of Islam in 1952, thus identifying himself with the group. He later became Minister Malcolm X Shabazz. After going on pilgrimage to Mecca and Africa in 1964 and his religious conversion from an American Islamic sect to a global Suni Islamic denomination, he became Minister El-Hajj Malik El-Shabazz. El-Hajj is 'the pilgrim', Malik is the Arabic equivalent of his American name Malcolm. El-Shabazz signified an ancient African tribe. His wife's name is Betty Shabazz and his four daughters are:

93

Attilah (gift), Qabillah (amiable), Ilyasah (f. of Ilyaas, Elijah) and Amilah (doer).

From a famous man whom I met once at the United Nations but did not really know to a woman familiar to me personally and one of my former students, Amida Salahuddin. She wrote for me an account of her recent conversion to Islam and changing her family names.

> My family is the first generation of African-American Muslims in America. I was born Sandra I. Moore. My parents are Fred Moore and Addie M. Moore. My mother moved to New York City in the 1950's. My two brothers and I eventually lived with her. Growing up in New York City during the 1950's and 1960's was eventful. In 1968 I joined the membership of the Nation of Islam. My name was changed to Sandra 17X. My two daughters Aishah and Khadijah were also given the names Aishah 16X and Khadijah 14X. In 1975 the Nation of Islam underwent a transition into traditional Islam or what is more commonly called Orthodox Islam. Imam Warith Deen Muhammed (Wallace Muhammad), the son of the late Honorable Elijah Muhammad, challenged and inspired our community to grow out of the womb of racism and separatism into Al-Islam as practised by Prophet Muhammad (PBUH).[4]

It was then that Sandra I. Moore became Amidah Salahuddin. Imam Warith Deen Muhammad awarded Islamic names to families who participated in Da'wah (calling others to Islam) in 1976 and Amida's family was one of many who received an invitation to meet and have dinner with him. Her husband's name was changed from Clifford 8X to Hamid Sharif, her daughter Khadijah's name remained unchanged. The second daughter Aishah's name was changed to Asia. As she tells it:

> The letters Ami-ah were given to me and I spoke to a Sheikh in the community who told me to choose a conso-

nant. I chose Amidah because of my supportive role within my family and community. Muslims of African descent indigenous to America chose to change either their surname and family names or just their family names. Some families chose not to legally change their names because of bureaucratic encumbrances with health and life insurance etc. Many families have had the birth certificates and other documents legally changed.[5]

Today she has six children and three grandchildren. Her children are Asia Sharif-Clark, Khadijah Sharif, Hamidah Sharif, Raymond Ortiz, Najeeb Salahuddin and Jamilah J. Muhammad; her grandchildren are Raven LaToya, Taliah and Tariq.

Amidah Salahuddin's name was officialy registered in New York City during the 1970's by Sister Latifah Nuri along with that of many other African-American Muslim families.

Sister Latifah Nuri, a Muslim African-American, tells me that American Muslims choose their names on the basis of the meanings they convey. They consult name books and their religious leaders to choose a personal name and surname that express what they would like to be. Women, she told me, were discouraged from calling themselves Nisaa 'women' and men were discouraged from using Khalifa 'successor' since neither is sufficiently meaning specific. This is quite different from my experience growing up in East Africa where the use of both Nisaa and Khalifa are widespread. The noun nisaa' is used in a compound noun as Khayrunnisaa' which translates as 'the best of women.' Khalifa, 'successor', is very widely used. Among its most prominent bearers was the Sultan of Zanzibar Protectorate from 1911-1960, His Highness Seyyid Khalifa bin Harub bin Thuwaini bin Sa'id bin Sultan Al-Said.

When I asked Salahuddin for a list of popular female Muslim African-American names she gave the following:

Aishah Muhammad
Alyah Abdur-Rahim
Amina Abdul Haqq
Amina Muhammad
Fatimah Abdul-Aziz
Hanan Abdus-Salaam
Ibaadah Abdul-Khaaliq
Kalimah Kamal
Lateefah Abdul-Jabbar
Majida Abdur-Rahim
Malika Abdul-Hameed
Nedra Najeeullah
Nishel Taufeeq
Rukiyyah Abdur-Rahim
Samirah Muhammad
Siddiqua Akbar
Tauheedah Madyun
Widad Abdullah
Zakiyyah Madyun
Zarifa Muhammad

Salahuddin's list of popular Muslim African-American male names was:

Abdul-Hakeem Muhammad
Abdul Hakim Sharif
Abdul-Haqq Muhammad
Abdul-Rahman Ali
Abdur-Rahim Hassan
Abu Salih Abdul-Alim
Akbar Muhammad
Bilal Salahuddin
Kareem Abdul-Jabbar
Malik Mahdi
Muhammad Sharif

Naim Ziyad
Nashid Karim
Omar El-Amin
Razi Hassan
Sultan Muhammad
Wali Mohammed
Yahya Shabazz

PERSONAL NAMES AND POLITICS

Name changes often reflect particular, perhaps exceptional, political and social circumstances. It is unlikely that Muslim Swahili parents will bestow upon their child a Christian name without a very good reason. A Swahili family where the children are named James, Jeffrey and Christine is almost certainly one in which one of the parents (usually but not always the father) is either a Christian African or a Christian European.

The adoption of European or Christian names by Muslim Africans began in East Africa during the colonial era when parents wished to provide a child with a western education in schools run by missionaries. These schools required that school children not use their native languages. They were therefore required to take on non-African names. Such imposed name and language changes are acts of cultural violence, enforcing a form of alienation that destroys a child's self-identity. It is ironic that a school, a place of learning where a child should develop a unique identity and knowledge as self enhancement, should serve to undermine the child, robbing him or her of identity.[6]

In the 1960's when the three East African nations, Kenya, Tanganyika and Uganda, gained their independence from the British and new African states were established, many youths with distinctively non-African names, Baluchi, Farsi or Indian, were not happy using them since they so clearly expressed Asian ethnicity and identity. They concealed their given names by using only initials or adopting nicknames.[7]

The 1991-92 Tanzania Directory has Isaac Abeid, Isaac Sleiman, James Ahmed, John Mussa, John Omari, Joji Juma, Jonas Juma, George Johari, John Hamisi and other Christian and Muslim name combinations.

We also hear tribal names combined with Muslim names such as Kaleza Bilali, Kakwaya Mustafa, Kangero Abdalla, Kafuku Muhammed, Masawe Hussein, Kaindu Hassan, Kapasi Fakhruddin and Kanjenga Rashid. From the Kenya Directory we find Muslim personal names combined with non-Muslim fathers' names. A few examples of this kind are Suleman Kuria, Mwanaidi Wambui, Farook Mungai, Ayub Muthui and Swaleh Gitau. All these changes illustrate a process of integration in a context of cultural contact and cultural adaptations. Similarly, members of the elite who were of Arab descent and carried family names which indicated their Arab heritage such as Riyaami, Kharuusi, and Barwani dropped their family names since these often referred to a place of origin, a trade or profession, a tribe, or an ancestor not in keeping with their nationalist aspirations for the new African nation.[8] These were not legislated or forced changes by the new governments but are of sociological and political importance to the individuals who feared loss of rights and suffering because of their names. Furthermore a name is a label that usually reveals belonging and membership in a group.

Asa G. Hillard III, who is a psychologist and educational counselor, and Fuller E. Calloway, Professor of Urban Education at Georgia State University, Atlanta, Georgia and who is an African-American has observed:

Colonizers and slave owners knew that to destroy our names was to weaken us as a people, to disorient us, to make us dependent, and to force us to wear the symbol of that dependence, alien names, for ever.

He further suggests that the taking of non-English names, or the manipulation of their presentation, may be regarded as a declaration of independence of a sort.[9]

    Jan R. Carew confirms this loss of identity:

> To rob people or countries of their name is to set in
> motion a psychic disturbance that can, in turn, create
> a permanent crisis of identity.[10]

    Since the 1960's with the movement for civil rights,
the African-American community in the United States has
begun to bestow African names on their children and on
themselves as a way of consciously regaining their lost identity and raising their consciousness that they are Blacks or
Africans and not Negroes. All the names they use are derived
from African languages. Most of these African language
names I discussed in my previous book,
What's in a Name. They have positive
meanings and can be read as a
response to the liberation slo-
gan of the 1960's 'Black is
Beautiful.' As I suggested
there, they also establish the
foundation for a distinctive value
system and in so doing communicate a political or social message to
American society at large.[11] An apt
example of the 60's is the pan-Africanist
and civil rights activist Stokely
Carmichael who changed his name to
Kwame Ture. Mr.Ture changed his name in
1978 to honor the first President of Ghana,
Kwame Nkrumah, the father of pan-Africanism
who died in 1972 and Ahmed Sekou Toure president of Guinea who died in 1984.[12]

    Vanessa Sebanakitta, an African-American mother of
two and a former student of mine, chose her children's
names after searching through many books. She named her
daughter Akilah Isoke Jendayi:

> to reflect the qualities I hoped for as well as my heart-

felt sentiments at having been blessed with the gift of life - Akilah Isoke Jendayi, she who uses reason, beautiful gift, and gives thanks.

The first name of Mrs. Sebanakitta's daughter comes from Arabic, the second is Nigerian and the third name is Shona.

Mrs. Sabanakitta's son is Kahlil Agyei, friend and messenger.

My son's name was also chosen after deep reflection into the meaning of his birth, and the hope that he will develop along the paths which his names suggest.[13]

NAMES AND PERSONAL ADVANCEMENT

Many immigrants change their names for economic reasons so as to overcome social and financial obstacles. A case of another former student and friend, Ali Brooks, is an appropriate example. His name reveals a combination of two languages and two different ethnicities. The first name is Arabic and the second English, a breaking down of language boundaries. The name Ali Brooks carries a deep cultural message. *'Ali*, the cousin and son-in-law of Prophet MuHammad, is revered as the fourth Khalifa of Islam and the father of the martyrs Hassan and Hussein, eminent Imams, (leaders), of the Shi'a sect.

But the father who named Ali Brooks apparently has a non-Islamic name just as apparently as the son bears a Muslim name.

One might think that the name Brooks was derived from an English name such as that of H.J. Brooke, the famous English mineralogist, or Rupert Brooke, the poet. The word comes from the Old English broc, a stream, and hence means 'someone who lives near a stream.' This is like the Urdu meaning of Nehru we saw earlier. Such names reflect common practice in early societies, where most people live and die where they are born, of identifying families by the localities in which they live.

The truth is even more interesting. Ali's father came from Iraq to the United States as a young man in 1954 looking for work and education. Like so many other immigrants, he had difficulty getting a job because of his difficult foreign-sounding name. It was S̲abiih Ali Al-Bahbahaan. The name was also a mouthful for his new acquaintances, and so Al-Bahbahan decided to change his Arabic name to that of one of his friends, Robert Brooks, thus adopting an English name. He did not choose it for its meaning, but for its familiarity. It was the name of someone to whom he could relate. S̲abiih̲ Bahbahaan did this to adapt to a new way of life and a new environment but also to overcome social and economic humiliation. His new name gave him recognition, jobs and respect. His Iraqi friends continued to call him S̲abiih̲, handsome, while his new friends called him Bobby. Ironically, Robert Brooks subsequently gave his children Muslim names, among them his son, my friend, Ali Brooks.

Forty years later, in 1995, Robert Brooks and the family changed their name back again to the original Arabic name of Bahbahaan. The change had marked a significant and serious phase in the immigrant's life: with security and, perhaps, confidence again in the openness of American society—and at the suggestion of his children growing up in a more tolerant multicultural times the family reverted to a wholly Arabic name as Arab-Americans.

HISTORICAL CHANGES

Not only do many people change their names, the meanings or contents of names may change over time and place. Hence there is a close connection between the name and what it designates within the context of time and place.

Here we may use a literary example. A well known Swahili folk hero is named Liongo or Liyongo. To any Swahili speaker who knows Swahili literature, this name evokes a famous celebrated Swahili hero, a warrior and poet, who is credited with composing many ancient Swahili poems going back to the 13th century or even earlier. The epic poem,

Utendi wa Liyongo, narrates the story of his life and it influenced and inspired many later verse compositions such as those of Muhammad bin Abubakar bin Umar al-Bakri (nicknamed Muhammad Kijuma), Muyaka bin Haji Al-Ghassany and Abdul Karim bin Jamaliddini.

Whether Liyongo was Christian or Muslim has led to heated discussions. The first documented description of Liyongo appeared in a Swahili manuscript published by the Rev. Edward Steere in 1870. Although there have been numerous intense debates published and unpublished as to the historical authenticity of the character and his identity, no one has attempted to explore the cultural content of his name and its significance. Let me do this now.

The Arabic root l-gh-w 'words' in the name Liyongo (as in its use in the Qur'aan to convey 'useless words')[14] designates a person who talks nonsense and behaves foolishly. The name is therefore derogatory and its root of -*ongo* in contemporary Swahili means a liar. However, Liyongo in contemporary Swahili literature is anything but foolish or a liar. The original negative characterization implied by the name has been changed over time and place. The new image was created by new users of the name Liyongo in a new African language, Swahili. Since we do not possess a documented account older than that of Steere in 1870 there is nothing to relate the old Arabic meaning of the name to the modern character.[15] This should not preclude a scholar from *associating* the original meaning of the word with the modern characterization of the same person. What seems to have changed is the message and the image given to the word. Those who first coined the name for Liyongo did not condone what he was saying and, for them, he was talking nonsense. This was the description, the content and the image presented by the early Arabic name. Today's Swahili poetry provides a different context and content and the name Liyongo now designates a well-liked, respected and admired folk hero. A positive image has replaced the negative one.[16]

Let us look at another example of the way in which

the users of a name determine its meaning within their own time and place. The title sayyid, sayad or sidi in Hausa-Fulani, seyyid in Kiswahili, in North Africa sidi or sayyid in classical Arabic has the common root s-y-d or s-w-d. The Arabic-English dictionary, The Hans Wehr Dictionary of Modern Written Arabic, edited by J.M.Cowan gives the following definitions:

s-y-d, siyaadah see s-w-d

1. s-w-d II. [i.e. form II sawwad] to make black, blacken, to draft a letter, bring into dispute, disgrace, dishonor...sawaad black color, blackness...aswad f. saudaa' pl. suud black

2. s-w-d, saada (siyaadah, su'dud, su'dad) to be or become master, head, chief...govern, Form II sawwad means to make master, head, chief...s-y-d sayyid pl. asyaad, saada, saadaat master, gentleman...title of Mohammed's direct descendants

3. sayyidii colloq. siidii) honorific before the names of Muslim Saints...sayyida pl. sayyidaat lady, Mrs...siyaada command, mastery...general title of respect preceding the name...su'dud, su'dad dominion, reign, power...saa'id prevailing[17]

In other dictionaries[18] the roots s-y-d/s-w-d have both meanings, blackness and chieftainship. In their contemporary usage, the two words are distinct one from each other, the one s-w-d indicating the color black used derogatively, and the other s-y-d indicating an honorific or title. Not only the spelling and the usage but the meanings have been defined within their new environment. The positive and negative connotations of each usage have been crystallized. What brought about the change and why and when did it occur? When did the meaning and the use of the word black become distinct from its meaning as leader or chief and when did it acquire pejorative meaning? Many types of 'leader' become characterized both negative and positive, witches and wiz-

103

ards are good and bad. This distinction is perhaps related to the color prejudice that resulted in the racial concept of white superiority and black inferiority of our time. A follow-up of the cursory analysis presented here would provide important socio-linguistic and historical insight.[19]

Several recent African examples of names that are in process of moving away from their original usages may be given from Tanzania and Kenya Directories. *Juma/Jum'ah* means Friday, the day Muslims congregate for prayer.[20] The same root means those who are related, a community, jamaa'a. *'id/Idd/Idi* means festivity and,in Africa, specifically a Muslim festivity after the fasting of the month of *Ramadhan/RamaDaan* or after the pilgrimage to Mecca. Both terms are frequently used by Muslims as names for children born on these days or to signify other happy occasions. They are also now widely used in East Africa by non-Muslims. In Kenya the name Juma appears in combination with non-Muslim names such as Gabriel, Hampton, John, Peter, Joseph, Kihiyo, Larry, Samson, Stephen and Maurice and in Tanzania with Jonas and Joji. Idi also appears in Tanzania with non-Muslim names.

Ismail/Isma'iil is the name of a prophet and in Islamic chronology the son of Ibrahiim (Abraham). This name appears four times with non-Muslim names. The fourth, Hawa, is a female name in traditional Swahili culture and symbolizes the wife of Adam. The name Hawa, together with female names such as Munira and Jamila, is used in Kenya fiction as masculine names besides their masculine counterparts, Munir, Adam and Jamil.

NEW NAMES

New and modern names keep surfacing all the time influenced by popular culture, films, songs, language and literature. A name such as Tarikhu Farrar, the history of the defector, expresses a contemporary message. Yet this is not a new fashion: from Nigeria we see names such as King, Prince, Saturday, Monday, Lucky and Christmas. African-

American slaves used to translate their similar African names into English. More recently in East Africa there are Robert Taylor, Sal Davies, Meri, Maria, (from Mariam/Mary), Nadiin, Ruby, Natasha, Samantha, Juliet, Janet, Julian, Rosy, and Sabrina. These are characters in English literature and some are equivalents or translations of indigenous concepts.[21] I mentioned before that one important source for a new name is a spouse. Intermarriages between different cultures bring fresh names.[22]

Young people sometimes change their names by shortening them to pet names: so MaHbuub/Mahboob becomes Bob, Adil becomes Del, Rahim becomes Roy, Daud becomes Dowd, Jannat becomes Janet, Latiif and LaTiifa become Tif and Tifa, Fatma becomes Fatu or Tuma, Salim becomes Sal, Kariim/Kareem becomes Kim, Ibraahim becomes Brahima, Bim or Imu, Abuubakar becomes Baker. Although these may not be the names their parents call them by, they are popular with their peer groups and friends. Parents also may have their own abbreviations which they use as terms of endearment, Fatu for Fatma, Su for Su'aad, Dosi for Firdaus, Ifa for Sharifa, Imu for Ibrahim. Some parents use the English word 'baby' as a nickname for their daughters.

It is too soon to assess whether these innovations will take in the different setting. It is, however, certain that, despite these recent fresh names appearing in the Swahili diaspora, the general trend among the masses, both those abroad and those still living in East Africa, is to duplicate their relatives' names which are passed down from one generation to another. They continue to use the historical and religious names long established in their communities.[23]

NOTES

1.   Conversion to Islam followed high status diplomatic contacts as may be seen also in England. Another example of a Muslim convert taking a Muslim name was Lord Headley al-Farooq formerly known as Rt.Hon.Sir Rowland George Allanson. He was

born in 1855. A leading British peer, statesman and author, became a Muslim in 1918 and adopted the Muslim name of Shaikh Rahmatullah al-Farooq.

2. 'My Journey' in *Islamic Horizons* Sept/Oct. 1995, p.24.

3. The organization of the Nation of Islam in the United States was founded by Wali Fard Muhammad in 1930 who disappeared in 1933. Its roots also go back to African-American nationalist leaders such as Edward W. Blyden, Nobel Drew Ali and Marcus Garvey.

4. The abbreviation stands for peace be upon him. It is SAAW in its Arabic equivalent.

5. Personal correspondence with 'Amidah Salahuddin, January 18, 1996.

6. See my discussion of Shaaban Robert and his name in *What's in a Name?* pp.15-17.

7. Personal conversation with Professor Jaffer Kassamali of Tanzania who now lives in New York City and teaches at Hunter College, CUNY.

8. See Zawawi, 1993: 5-6.

9. See the Foreword in Nia Damali, 1986.

10. Ibid., the back cover of the same book.

11. See Zawawi (1993: 27-36) on this discussion and for a list of some of these names.

12. Kwame or Kwami is an Akan name for one born on a Saturday. I discussed the Ghanaian custom of calling a child by his or her day of birth in my previous book. See p. 78.

13. Personal correspondence January, 1996.

14. The Suras where the name is to be found is Al-Shu'araa (The Poets), Sura 26 verse 224: As for poets, the erring follow them and Al-QaSas (Stories), Sura 28 verse 18: Moses told him: You are clearly a trouble-maker.

15. In Swahili the root ongo means to tell a lie.

16. A similar but reverse attitude is the name of the first President of a free India, Jawahar lal Nehru that I mentioned in chapter three of this book. Salman Rushdie, a famous English writer of Indian origin in his latest book uses this name to designate a dog in his fiction. This has angered many Indians who have a different image of their President. How Rushdie regards a dog will symbolize the intended significance and attitude of such naming. An earlier resentment was expressed in relation to the characters

and their names which Rushdie symbolizes in his *Satanic Verse*.

17. p. 440.
18. See E.W.Lane, *Arabic English Lexicon*, 1863. Lane derives sawwad from the root s-w-d, i.e. chief, lord, master or possessed of glory, honor, dignity, eminence, etc. He illustrates its meaning in a sentence: Sawwadahu qawmuhu 'His people made him a sayyid i.e. a chief or lord.' See also J.G. Hava, *Al-Faraid Arabic-English Dictionary*, Beirut, 1970.
19. The role of blacks in ancient civilization is examined by Cheikh Anta Diop in his discussion on Kemit (Egypt). See his book on *Black Civilization*. The works of Martin Barnal, Molefi Kete Asante and Ali Mazrui provide additional information.
20. It is Al-Jum'ah in Arabic and Ijumaa in Kiswahili.
21. The actor Omar Shariff's personal name Omar is popular in the United States among Spanish men. Farid, an Egyptian singer, provides a popular name in East Africa.
22. For some examples see Zawawi, 1993, p. 19.
23. Ibid. p. 20.

CHAPTER SEVEN

AFRICAN NAMES AND MEANINGS

Jina lisilo maana ni nyumba isiyo msingi.

A name without meaning is like a house without
a good foundation. (Swahili proverb)

This chapter examines African Muslim names, their form
and content, their linguistic adaptation and synthesis, and
their spelling and pronunciation. Examples of crosscultural
adaptations are also discussed. The names used by two
groups of Africans are presented in this chapter. They are
the Hausa-Fulani of West Africa and the Waswahili of East
Africa. Lists of African Muslim names are preceded by a discussion of the sociolinguistic contexts necessary for understanding their significance. These names, masculine and
feminine, are drawn from three different sources and
arranged in alphabetical order at the end of the chapter.

Olowa O. Ojoade lists twelve categories of traditional African Yoruba names, giving the following types:

1) Lineage names
2) Names of royalty
3) Place names
4) Names of events
5) Occupational names

6) Stereotyped names
7) Nicknames
8) Day names
9) Names derived from gods or goddesses and natural phenomena
10) Names derived from titles, hereditary and non-hereditary
11) Praise names
12) Proverbial names reduced or derived from proverbs.[1]

All but the last two of these categories are also to be found among the Waswahili.[2] They also categorize the Muslim names discussed in Chapters Three and Four.
African names are derived from three sources:
1) Indigenous African names
2) Muslim African names
3) Christian African names
Origins are not always clear since over the centuries population movement, migration, mobility and intermarriage have transformed ethnic and tribal settlements, effacing social boundaries. Nevertheless, the recognition of three distinct sources is useful when discussing how particular social histories have defined African identities.
According to Nyang, Professor of African Studies at Howard University, the African man sees himself as a citizen of three different worlds at the same time:
a) the world of concrete reality
b) the world of social values
c) the world of ineffable self-consciousness.[3]
Nyang's three worlds therefore require cultural awareness and self-identity and names express this.

AFRICAN MUSLIM NAMES

All the different types of names that I discussed in Chapter Three as Islamic - the ism (the personal name), the kunya or tekonym (Abu/Umm father/ mother or belonging to), the laqab (Name+diin), the nasab (family or clan name) and nisba (place of origin)- appear in Hausa-Fulani and

Kiswahili as will be seen from the lists below. Any changes that appear are linguistic and due to adaptations of these names to African languages and cultures.

The Islamic nomenclature in both regions of Africa is based on God's name, Allah, on God's attributes, names of prophets and Prophet MuHammad's family members and associates and on the Islamic calendar and astrology. The secular names convey chronology of birth, titles, regional affiliation, descriptive qualities and historical identities and connections. The changes seen between names from Africa and those of the rest of the Islamic world are grammatical.

ISLAMIC NAMES USED BY THE HAUSA-FULANI AND THE SWAHILI

This section examines African Muslim names and makes two comparisons:
1) African Muslim names with Arabic Muslim names
2) Hausa-Fulani names with Swahili names

A comparison of African Islamic names with Arabic Islamic names affirms the following usage:

1. An African Muslim son or daughter has a personal name followed by a paternal name, the father's, and then the grandfather's.[4] This familial relationship is indicated in Arabic by the word *ibn* or *bin*, 'son of' or *bint*, 'daughter of.' Swahili speakers use the exact particles.

Hausa-Fulani speakers use *bin* as in Abdullah *bin* Fadio but also use an indigenous particle *dan* or its abbreviation *da* (m.) and yar (f.) meaning 'child of.' Thus the Fulani Muslim scholar who founded the Sokoto caliphate was called Shehu/Sheikh Usman/'Uthman dan Fodio. Since Abdullah bin Fodio was the brother of Shehu 'Uthman dan Fodio we may assume that at this period (c.A.D. 1750-1820) there was no strict rule about which usage should be adopted.[5]

The particle dan 'son of' combines with different categories as illustrated in the following examples:
dan + personal name as in Ali dan Musa
dan + place name as in Ali dan Zaria

111

dan + ethnic group as in Ali dan Fulani
dan + title as in Ali Danshehu
dan + tekonym as in Ali Danbaba
dan + occupation as in Ali dan Najjar
dan + description as in Ali Danbaha

2. In addition to the two particles bin and dan, Hausa-Fulani speakers may use with their names *Mai* or its shorter form *Ma*, meaning 'owner/of.' Some examples are Maijama (one born on a Friday), Mailafia (one born healthy), Mai Kano (one from the city of Kano), Maigida 'head of the house'.[6] Other particles in Hausa that combine with a personal name are *ba* 'person' as in Ali+Ba, or Balarabe/Balaraba 'person born on Wednesday'. In Arabic Ba occurs with tribal names as in Baalawy, Baharuun and BaSheikh.

Na (m.) and *ta* (f.) meaning 'belonging to, of' as in Na/Tabiyu 'the following, second one.'

3. Both Hausa-Fulani and Waswahili use chronological numbering for personal names as for example in:

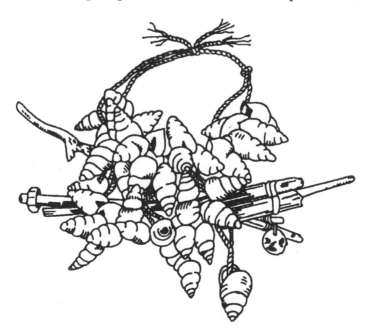

112

English	Arabic	Hausa-Fulani	Swahili
First	Awwal[7]	Lawal/Danlaw	Mosi
Second	Thaany	Sani	Pili
Third	Thaalithu	Salisu	Tatu
Fourth	Raabi'u	Rabi'u/Rabiu	Nne
Fifth	Khaamis	Hamisi/Khamis	Tano/
			Hamisi[8]

Note how the two languages relate in closeness to the Arabic word. The Hausa speaker retains the original form of the word but changes its pronunciation and, as a result, its spelling. The Swahili speaker, on the other hand, translates the Arabic word into its Swahili equivalent.

4. Both Hausa-Fulani and Waswahili name their children according to their day of birth, bestowing on them the following names:

English	Arabic	Hausa-Fulani	Swahili
Saturday	Al-Sabt	Danasabe (m.)	Mosi (f+m.)
		(Yar)Asabe (f.)	Sebtu (f.)
Sunday	Al-AHad	Danlahadi/Danladi	Pili
Monday	Al-Ithnayn	Altine/Tine	Tatu
Tuesday	Al-thalaatha	Talata (m.)Talatu (f.)	Jumaane
Wednesday	Al-Arba'a	Balarabe/Alaraba (m.)	Machano/Matano
		Balaraba (f.)	
Thursday	Al-Khamiis	Hamis/Alamisu	Khamis/Hamisi
			Mwana Hamisi
Friday	Al-jum'a	Danjuma (m.)	Juma/Adam
		Jummai (f.)Adam (m.)	Mwajuma[9]
		Adama/Hawwa	

It may be seen that both Hausa-Fulani and Swahili have masculine and feminine forms for some of the days.

5. Hausa-Fulani speakers customarily attach place names to their personal names. Examples of this include: Musa Zaria or Musa dan Zaria, Muhammadu (dan) Kano,

Ilyasu (dan) Katsina, Rahman (dan) Hadejia, Liman (dan) Daura and Haruna (dan) Gombe. It is not so common among the Waswahili to use their names in combination with a place of origin but they do use location in conversation when they need to identify a person.

6. Neither Hausa-Fulani women nor Waswahili women have to drop their fathers' and family names for those of their husbands upon marriage. Nevertheless (as we have seen), some of the more Westernized women do.[10] African Muslim women's right to use their own names after marriage goes together with their right to own and sell property, to enter into business contracts and to perform other legal transactions independently of their husbands. Nevertheless, Muslim women of both African and Arabic descent have not been able to take full advantage of this legal right.

It could be argued that their contribution to society has not been fully realized not because of any religious systems but because of economic and political conditions in their social and cultural environments.

7. African Muslim names, like Arabic Islamic names, are either preceded or followed by titles as in Alhaji Sir Abubakar Tafawa Balewa, Prime Minister of Nigeria from 1960-1966 or Alhaji Aliyu Shehu Shagari, President of Nigeria from 1979-1983. It has been easy to identify the names of Muslims from the northern states such as Sokoto, Katsina, Kano, Bauchi and Kaduna because they are followed by an abbreviated title of Alh. for a man and Alha. for a woman. These stand for Alhajj and Alhajja respectively. It is most likely that the title here stands for a Muslim rather than specifically for someone who has performed a pilgrimage to Mecca. Hausa-Fulani customs of address are more formal and complex than those of the Waswahili but they do have several in common, e.g. al-hajj, mu'allim/mwalimu, shariff and sheikh/shehe/sheha. The Hausa-Fulani system of ranking people by their official positions is known as *sarauta* and is both old and elaborate. Titles signifying rank or kinship

terms embellish names even when friends address one another. Two Hausa proverbs express the views of their users:

Abookin sarki sarkii nee.

A chief's friend is a chief.

Allah shi ne sarki.

God is the Chief of chiefs.

Although to a certain extent this custom of using titles is changing slowly, the best advice to give a visitor to the country is always to use a title when addressing an associate unless one is invited to drop it!

Hausa-Fulani *sarauta* indicates lineage, prestige, authority, status, class, respect, profession and acknowledgment. They are used to designate royal, administrative, religious and political leadership. They involve the use of classificatory titles derived from both Arabic and indigenous terminology such as *sarkii* (chief, king, emir, leader of profession) and *sarauniyaa*, its female equivalent.

Those of Islamic origin include the following:

Alhaji	he who has been on pilgrimage to Mecca or a Muslim man, e.g. Alhaji Ibrahimu or Ibrahimu Alhaji
Al-Haja	she who has been on pilgrimage to Mecca or a Muslim woman, e.g. Al-haja Khadijatu
Amir/Emir	prince as in Emir of Kano, Alhaji Abdullahi Bayero (1929-1953). His other title is Mai Tattabaru.
Al-kali/ Gadi	judge of shari'a law, e.g. Ibrahim Al-kali
Hakimi	district head, wise man

Imam/Iman	leader e.g. Imam Tijani
Khalifa	head of Islamic community
Ma/Mallam/Malam	religious teacher, now used for Muslims and Christians e.g. Mallam Aminu
Malama	a woman religious teacher e.g. Malama Rukaiyatu
Mufti	consultant of shari'a, the Islamic law
Sayad	Mr. or descendant of Prophet MuHammad
Sherif/Sharif	noble, descendant of Prophet MuHammad
Sheikh/Shaikh/	leader, e.g. Shehu Shagari Shehu
Sidi	abbreviated form of Sayyid, Mr. or descendant of Prophet MuHammad e.g. Sidi Abdulkadiri
Sultan	ruler, as in Sultan Mansa Musa the ruler of Mali or Amir Sultan Muhammad Bello of Sokoto (1739-1837)
Waly/Wali	governor, sage or saint
Wazir	grand vizier, Prime Minister, or advisor of the amir

These titles and their rankings vary from region to region within West Africa and in some cases their spellings differ, too. Although their use to distinguish classes goes back many centuries and is endorsed by its patrons, in modern times it is resented by the commoners and the less privileged who have to compete against it. Contemporary social attitudes brought about by modern education, social mobility, urbanization, the mass media and political developments are rendering these titles less significant and consequently challenging their owners' political and economic power. Some titles are also used as personal names. Those that appear[11] to be used in this way include Waziri, Imam and its variant Iman, Shehu, Sheriff and Wakili. Waswahili use some

116

of these titles too in addition to Mwinyi, Makame, Mfalme, Mfaume, Fumo, Haji, Mzee, Babu, Ustadh and Bwana for men and Siti, Somo, Mwana, Nyanya, Bibi, Bibiye, Mama, Hababa, Nana, Haboo for women when addressing one another.

SPELLING AND PRONUNCIATION OF HAUSA-FULANI AND SWAHILI MUSLIM NAMES

The African spelling of Muslim names is disadvantaged when the names are written in English script. This is because sounds that do not appear in the English language or alphabet cannot be represented.[12] Sounds which linguists term emphatic consonants, such as Saad (   ), Daad (   ), Taa (   ), Zaa (   ) and the pharyngals 'ayn (   ) and Haa (   ) and the glottal stop '(   ) cause most difficulty. These sounds appear in the following names:

'ali and 'aliyya
Hasan and Hasnaa
KhiDr and FaDiila
Sanaa' and Aalaa'
SalaaH, SalHa
Taariq and FaaTima
Zaahir and Zahiira

There are four ways in which these sounds may be represented in the spelling used in English script:

1) The sound may be dropped or a substitute used instead. Using the English (Roman) equivalent and simply writing them as: s, d or dh, t, z and k as in

117

Salah for SalaaH, Fadila or Fadhila for FaDiila, Taha or Twaha for Taaha and Aziim for 'AZiim, Faika for Faaiqa, Halili for Khaliil.[13]

2) Dropping the 'ayn and using the vowel that follows it as in Ali for 'Ali, Asad for As'ad, Shuaib for Shu'ayb, Umar for 'Umar and Said for Sa'iid.

Leaving out the glottal stop as in Hana for Hanaa' and in Sana for Sanaa' or replacing it with a y as in Nayla for Naa'ila

3) The sound may be represented by writing the equivalent English letter and adding a dot or a line under it to indicate that it differs in pronunciation from the English sound e.g. 'Ataa, Azhar, Taaha, Safiya

4) The sound may be presented by writing the equivalent in English with a capital letter as in AHmad, FaDila, MuHammad, MaHbuuba and HaafiZ.

The choice of which set of symbols or diacritical marks is used varies from one writer to another.

VOWEL LENGTH

The spelling of names in English script does not always represent the original vowel length in Arabic. There are many examples of this nature:

Afiya is used for 'Aafya or 'Afiiya

Ali is used for 'Ali or 'Alii

Sadiki is used for Saadiq or Sadiiq

Salim is used for Saalim or Saliim

The Arabic vowels may be represented in several different ways in English script:

1) by ignoring length and writing one close to it as in Khadija instead of Khadiija

Sharifa instead of Shariifa

118

2) by doubling the vowels as in Muniir, Sa'iid, Aqeel 'Aqiil, FaDiila, NuuH, MaHmuud, Yuusuf, Nuur, and Muusa

3) by writing a line on top of the equivalent vowel to indicate length as in Salim, Said

DROPPING OF CERTAIN CONSONANTS

Another feature which results in name variations is the dropping of one of the consonants from an Arabic name. Thus:
1) dropping of H in the following names:

Hanifa becomes Anifa
MuHammadu becomes Momodou
Habiiba becomes Abiiba
Habibu becomes Abibu
Ahmed becomes Amadu
Saleh becomes Sale
Salahu becomes Salau
Mahmuud becomes Mammud or Mamood
Al-Hasan becomes Alasani
Harun sometimes becomes Arun
Sahibu becomes Saibu

2) dropping a final consonant in the following names:

'Abdul becomes Abdu
'Abbuud becomes Abu
Adam/Adamu becomes Ada
'Antar becomes Anta[14]
Dan-mulak becomes Damulak
Umari becomes Umai
Yusuf becomes Yusu
Zakariya becomes Zakari/Zaka

3) dropping other consonants in names that are long:

Abdulkarim becomes Abdularim
Abdulqadir becomes Abdukadiri or Abdulkad
Suleman becomes Sule

4) The change of m to n when it occurs in a final position:

Abdulsalam becomes Abdulsalani
Imam becomes Iman

5) The change of l to n in the final position

Jibril becomes Jibrin
Lawal becomes Iawan

Again, the Arabic sounds of these names are handled differently by different authors. Hence on reading any text it is useful first to note the key symbols used by the author in order to understand his intended presentation of the various sounds. When cataloging Muslim names the question of how to spell them in English poses a problem for the librarian and for those who use the library. Yet, being able to pronounce a name correctly is important both to the person who uses the name and to the one named.

ARABIC GRAMMATICAL ELEMENTS AFFECTING AFRICAN NAMES CASE ENDINGS

When African Muslim names are compared with Arabic Muslim names, the differences encountered in pronunciation are also the result of grammatical features which occur in the Arabic language. Take the name 'Abd, for instance. This appears in Arabic in different grammatical contexts as 'Abdu, 'Abda and 'Abdi as in:

Huwa 'Abdu+llah (He is Abdullah, nominative).

Raayt 'Abda+llah (I saw Abdallah, accusative).

120

Takallamt ma'a 'Abdi+llah (I talked to Abdillah, after a preposition).

Similarly Ab appears as Abu, Aba and Abi as in Abu Bakar, Aba Bakar, and Abi Bakar;'Umar has 'Umaru, 'Umara, and 'Umari. Some names have only two case endings -u and -a as in the following names: Ibraahiim has Ibraahiimu and Ibraahiima, Haruun has Haarunu and Haruna, Yusuf has Yusufu and Yusufa, Daud has Daudu and Dauda.

An Arabic language text is written without vowels. The only text where vowels must be included so as to prevent misreading is the Qur'aan. No text has influenced African Muslim literature more than the Qur'aan since it presents to its readers all the grammatical features possible in Arabic. Since the case ending is dropped in Arabic whenever one pauses, the vowel ending is not heard or written and so the name is pronounced simply as Adam, Ibraahiim, Yusuf, Haruun, Ya'quub, and Umar. In Hausa-Fulani speech one hears both Ibrahimu and Ibrahima. In choosing names for their children Hausa-Fulani Muslims vocalize names with the back vowel u thus: Adamu, Aliyu, Aminu, Daudu, Ilyasu, Kabiru, Muniru, Nafiu, Sadiku, Saidu, Salihu, Shaibu

Yakubu, Yusufu. They also have Adama, Ahmada, Dauda, Haruna, Ismaila, Nura and Umara, as well as Abdi, Amini, Daudi, Ismaili, Kabiri, Umari and Yusufi. This is the effect of the written text on the pronunciation of the name.

Waswahili in most cases tend to drop the final vowel and instead write and pronounce these names as Adam, Amin, Daud/Dawood,[15]Haruun, Ibraahim, Iliyas, Said, Saleh, Shaib, 'Umar, Yusuf and so on. This is the way they are pronounced in Arabic. A few cases of the -i ending appear as variants in names such as Ahamadi, Daudi and Umari. A possible explanation for the Swahili pronunciation may be that it was less influenced by written texts. The Waswahili had more intimate contact with Arabs and thus greater knowledge of the Arabic way of pronouncing these names. The variations in Hausa may also be the result of Hausa-Arabic contact with other African Arabs via Tuareg, Songhay, Mandingo, Kanuri besides the Classical Arabic, Swahili-Arabic contact was only with southern Arabic dialects and the Classical Arabic of the Qur'aan.

THE FEMININE SUFFIX

Another feature that causes variations in some Muslim names is the appearance of a feminine suffix. In Arabic script feminine names which end with -t marbuuTa, are written with a closed {-t}.[16] When the name is said and nothing follows immediately after it, the [-t] sound is dropped and what is heard at the end of the name is the vowel sound -ah/a. A good example is Amiinatun with the full suffix. Without it, it becomes Amiina in Arabic speech. This type of name may be spelt in several ways, i.e. Amina, Aminah, Aminat, Aminatu and Aminata. It may also be spelt Amiina, lengthening the middle stressed vowel for correct pronunciation. All these forms refer to the same word.

If a name is part of a compound in Arabic as in Amiinatu-Ssa'adiyya, the feminine ending is pronounced in especially slow, clear speech. Hausa-Fulani speakers treat this ending differently, the name appearing as Amiinatu or Aminata rather than Amiina. Other examples include Hafsat instead of HafSa, Khadiijatu instead Khadiija, Rukaiyatu instead of Ruqaya, and Aishatu instead of 'Aisha. The Swahili version of the same name is closer to the Arabic pronunciation dropping the feminine suffix. The names are simply: Amiina, HafSa, Khadija, Ruqaya or Rukiya and Asha or Esha. The Hausa-Fulani use sex gender suffixes even on names that do not have gender equivalents in classical Arabic and Kiswahili. A few examples include Adam (m.)and Adama (f.), Hasan (m.) and Hasana (f.), Balarabe (m.) and Balaraba (f.). Hausa-Fulani is thus close to the Arabic text in the use of masculine and feminine gender in many of the names.[17]

ABBREVIATING A NAME

Further variations besides those due to case and gender endings occur in Hausa-Fulani Muslim names. Other spelling modifications appear as a result of simplifying or abbreviating a name by dropping one of its consonants:

For a combination of Abdu+Allah the following variations occur:

Abdullahi Abullahi, Abdullah, Abdalla, Abdulai, Abdul, Abdu and Abdi. For the name Abubakar there are the following variations:

Abubakar, Abubakari, Aboubacar, Abubaka, Ababakar, Abubamcar, Adubakari, Abou Baker, Bakari, Bakare, Bakar, Bukar and Abu.

For the name MuHammad there are the following variations:

Muhammada, Muhammadi, Hammadi, Muhammadu, Muhammad, Muhammed, Muhamed, Mohammed, Mohammad, Mohammadu, Mamadoum, Mahammadu, Mamam, Mamman, Momodu, Muomah, Mohmodu, Mohd, Muomah, Momoh, Mamadou, Mamadu, Momo, Mame, Mordi, Mudi, Moha, and Moh. There are the following variations for the name AHmad:

Ahmadu, Ahmadou, Ahmed, Ahmad, Ahmada, Ahmadi, Amadu and Amadi.

There are the following variations for the name 'Aliyyu: Alliyu, Allyu, Aliyu, Aliu, Alioune.

There are the following variations for the name 'Umar: Umar, Umaru, Umari, Umara, Omari, Omar, Omoru, Umoru.

All these examples show that Hausa-Fulani speakers maintain case endings but abbreviate the names.

A COMPARISON OF ARABIC HAUSA-FULANI AND SWAHILI MUSLIM NAMES[18]

The following is a comparison of some common Arabic Islamic names as they appear in Hausa-Fulani and Kiswahili:

Arabic	Hausa-Fulani	Kiswahili
Aadam	Adamu/Adama/Adam/ Adu/Ado	Adam/Adamu
'Aashuur	Ashiru	Ashur
'Abbaas	Abas/Aba	Abasi/Abass/Abbas
'Abdallah	Abdulah/Abdallah	Abdalla/Abdulla
'Abdul	Abdul/Abdu	Abdul/Abduli
'Abdul'aziiz	Abdulaziz	Abdulaziz
'Abdulhaadi	Abdel-Hadi	Abdilhadi
'Abdulkariim	Abdulkarim	Abdulkarim
'Abdullah	Abdullahi	Abdillah
'Abdulmalik	Abdulmalik	Abdulmalik
'Abdulmun'im	Abdulmumun	Abdulmunim
'Abdulqaadir	Abdulkadir/ Abduljadir	Abdulkadir
'Abdulwahaab	Abdulwahab	Abdulwahab
'AbdurraHiim	Abdulrahim	Abdulrahim
'Abdurrazzaaq	Abdulrazak	Abdulrazak
'Abdussalaam	Abdulsalami	Abdulsalam
Abuubakar	Abubakar/Bukari	Abubakar/Bakari
'Abuud	Aboud/Abu	Abud/Aboud/Abbod
AHmad	Ahmadi/Ahmada	Ahmad/Ahmada
AHmad	Amadi/Amadou	Hamadi
AHmed	Ahmed	Ahmed/Ahmedi
'Ali	Ali	Ali
'Aliyyu	Aliyu/Alliyu	Aliy
Amiin	Aminu	Amin/Amini
Amiina	Aminatu	Amina
'Aqiil	Akilu	Akili
ATTaahir	Atahiru/Attahiru/ Tahir	Atta
Ayyuub	Ayubu/Ayuba	Ayub/Ayubu

124

Bashiir	Bashir/Bashiru	Bashir
Dawud	Dauda/Daudu	Daud/Daudi
Faaruuq	Faruk	Faruk
Habiib	Habib/Abibu	Habib/Habibu
HafSa	Hafsatu/Hafsa	Hafsa
Hajji	Hadji/Hajji	Haji
Hamza	Hamza	Hamza
Haruun	Haro/Aruna/	Harun/Haruni/
Haroun/Haruna	Haruna	
Hasan	Hassani/Hassan	Hasan/Hasani
Hawaa'	Hawa	Hawa
Hussain	Hoseni/Husen	Husen/Hussen
Ibraahiim	Ibrahim/Braimo	Ibrahim
'Iidd	Idi	Idi
Idriis	Idris/Idi	Idris
'Isaa	Isa/Isah	Isa
Ismaa'iil	Ismaila/Ismailu/	Ismail/Esmail
		Ismail
Ja'ffar	Jaafaru/Gaffar	Jaffar
Jamaal	Jammal/Jamali	Jamal
Jamiil	Jamil	Jamil
Kariim	Kareem/Karimi	Karim/
Khadija	Khadijatu/Kedia/	Khadija/Hadija/
Hadijatu	Katija	
Khaliil	Khalilu/Halilu	Khalil/Khalili
Khamiis	Hamis	Khamis/Hamis
LaTiif	Lateef/Latif	Latif
Maalik	Maliki/Malik	Malik

MaHmuud	Mamudu/Mahmud	
Mahmud/Mahmoud	Mahmood	Mahmood
Maliik	Maliki	Malik
Manqal	Manga	Manga
ManSuur	Mansor	Mansur/
		Mansour
Mas'uud	Mashood	Masud/Masudi
MuHammad	Muhammed/Mamadi	Muhammed[19]
Mukhtaar	Mukhtar/Muhtar	Mukhtar/
		Muhtari
Muniir	Muniru	Munir
Muusaa	Musa	Musa
MusTafa	Mustapha/	
Mustafa		Mustafa
NuuH	Nuhu	Nuuh
Nuur	Nura	Nuru
Qaadir	Kadiri	Kadiri
Qaasim	Kashimu/Kassimu	Kasim
Raashid/Rashiid	Rasheed	Rashid
RamaDaan	Ramadhan/Ramalan/	Ramadhani/
	Labran	Ramadhan
Sa'ad	Saad	Sadi
SaaliH	Salihu	Saleh/Salah
Saalim	Salim	Salim
Saamii	Sami	Sami
Sadiiq	Sadiku/Sadiq	Sadiki
Sa'iid	Saidu/Said	Said/Saeed
Salaam	Salami	Salam
Shaaib	Shaibu	Shaib
Sha'baan	Shaban/Bawa	Shaban/
		Shaabani
Suleimaan	Suleiman/Sule	Slemani/
		Sleman
Taahir	Tahir	Tahir
Taalib	Talabi	Talib
Tijani	Tijani	Tijani
'Umar	Umaru/Umara	Umar/Omar[20]

'Uthmaan Uthman/Usman/	Uthman/Othman[21]	Osman
Wakiil	Wakili/Wakeel	Wakili
Waziir	Waziri	Waziri
YaHya	Yahaya/Yahya	Yahya
Ya'quub	Yakubu/Kubu	Yakub/Yakubu
Yuunus	Yunusa/Yunus	Yunus
Yuusuf	Yusuf/Yusufu	Yusuf
Zakariyya	Zakari/Zaka	Zakaria
Zubair	Zubair	Zuberi

From this comparison of Muslim names in Arabic, Hausa-Fulani and Swahili, it can be seen that there are fewer abbreviated names in Swahili than in Hausa-Fulani. Take, for instance, the name MuHammad which in Swahili is MuHammed, Muhamadi, Mohammed, or in its abbreviated form Hamadi, Modi or Edi. The 1991-92 Tanzania telephone directory gives the first three variations. The Nigeria telephone directory, on the other hand, gives twenty- seven variations of MuHammad. Aisha or Aissatou is abbreviated Astou, Zainab, Nabou and Habiba, Aby. Because of the variations, the same person may appear in two or three different listings according to how the name is spelt. The name 'Uthman for instance, is listed under Uthman, Usman, Usuman, Usmanu, Usumanu, Usmang and Osman. Similarly 'Umar is listed under Umar, Umaru and Omar. Both Hausa-Fulani and Swahili speakers use the definite article al- with some of the names. Hausa-Fulani have Almustafa, Alhasan or Altahiru (Attahiru) and Swahili speakers have Al-Hasany, Al-Jabry, Al-Kariim, Al-Junaid, Al-Ameer, Al-Kindy and Al-Nashir. The definite article in Swahili is used with family names while in Hausa it appears with personal names.

The use of nicknames known in Hausa-Fulani as lak-abu and in Arabic as laqab is more predominant in Hausa-Fulani than in Swahili. Many names in Hausa-Fulani have nicknames, epithets or shortened forms of the same name. For instance, a boy named Abubakar is also Sadauki from

Abubakar Siddiiq, the companion of the Prophet MuHammad who was nicknamed 'the truthful one.' He may also be nicknamed Gagare, 'the powerful.' Yusufu which is equivalent to Joseph has a nickname Maitama or Mainasaru, 'the victorious.' He may also be called Mbaye. Ibraahim (Abraham) is nicknamed Shigari (Cigari) 'the conqueror' relating to Ibrahim, the ruler of Kano. The girl called Bilqiis or Bilkisi is nicknamed Gado 'the bed or throne' on which Bilqiis, the African queen, was sitting when she met Sulaymaan (Solomon).

Those named after their fathers or uncles are nicknamed Abba or Baba to avoid mentioning the name of an elder. In Swahili Babu 'grandfather' is a nickname for the one named after his grandfather. In speaking to her husband of someone of the same name the wife will refer to him as his namesake. The husband will also not use his wife's name.

The Hausa-Fulani list gives mostly male names as these are the names of fathers or grandfathers in a patrilineal society. Few women appear in the directory. On the other hand, the occurrence of female personal names such as Fatma, Aisha/Aysha, Khadija/Hadija, Mariam/Maryam, Salma and Amina are abundant in the Tanzania directory. This may indicate the role of women in the two regions and shows their limited participation in the official job market in the Hausa-Fulani region.

The frequency of names such as Kadiri, Tijani, Sanusi, Ali Shazili and Rifai in Nigeria reminds one of important leaders and founders of Sufi Tariqas, brotherhood fraternities such as the Qadiriyya and the Tijaniyya that had come from North Africa via Mauritania to Mali and Kano in Nigeria in the 14th century. These names recall some of the leaders responsible for introducing Islamic education to Africa. They are 'Abd-al-Qaadir al-Jiilaani (1077-1166), Ahmad al-Rifaa'i (d.1183), MuHyi-al-diin ibn 'Arabi (1165-1240), 'Ali al-Shaadhili (d.1258), Ahmad al-Tijaani (d. 1815), and Sidi MHammad ibn 'Ali al-Sanuusi (d. 1859).

Hausa-Fulani and Swahili parents choose these historic persons for their children's names. Another historic name in this region is Baba which goes back to a Muslim leader of Kumasi, MuHammad al-Ghaba', who was nicknamed Baba, 'the father.' The name Sunni may relate to Ali Ber, Ali the Great, also known as Sunni 'Ali who reigned in Songhay from A.D.1465-1492. It may also refer to another ruler Abu Bakar Da'u who was known as Sunni Barou. Askia is an honorific military title of the kings of Songhay. The famous Askia Alhaji Muhammad bin Abi Bakar of Ture who reigned between A.D.1493-1528 provides the name Askia. The many uses of Bello relate to the ruler of Sokoto. If therefore the literal meaning of names is of less importance today, their historical significance should not be overlooked.

Islamic Arabic names adapt to African languages and culture. For the meaning of a name to be intelligible and without ambiguity it must be correctly spelt to convey the original. Names are meaningless labels to someone who is not familiar with the language since they are formed in words that are derived from a language, but they are also of less significance when one is unaware of the social setting in which they occur.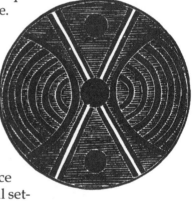

The content of a name may change according to the time and place which provide its context. The African language conveys its form and the users give it its reference and significance. Hence the language of contact is more than a means of verbal communication, it is indeed a symbol of group identity and a tool of understanding its culture.

These two African regions of Hausa-Fulani and Swahili communities have an enormous wealth of common names which have been in use for centuries and are still widely used. Not only do these names reflect their cultural distinctiveness and Pan-African identity, their rich meanings inculcate and preserve human values.

There will be a multitude of analyses and interpretations on the significance of names which are derived from the mystical power of words. The knowledge of the Arabic language that has influenced this culture is a key to its insights. Writers select data available to them and substantiate them with experience and prejudices. This study should be followed by further research that may fill the gaps and refine the analysis.

In the music of the universe
each shall give a different sound,
but necessary to the grand symphony.[22]

PART TWO

HAUSA-FULANI MUSLIM MALE NAMES

This list includes names that have appeared in previous chapters but sometimes vary in their spellings. The meaning is here provided in parentheses for those names that have not appeared in the text.

Abba, Abbas/Abashe, Abboud, Abdalah/Abdallah/Bdallah, Abdu/Abdul, Abdulateef, Abdulhamed/Abdulhameed/Abdulhamid, Abdukadir/ Abdukadiri/ Abdulkadir/ Abdukadir/Abduljadir/Abakadir, Abdulai/Abdullahi, Abdulkareem/ Abdulkarim, Abdulazeez/Abdulaziz/ Abdul-Aziz, Abdulladin, Abdull-Salami, Abdulmalik, Abdulmumin/ Abdulmumini, Abdulraham, Abdulrasaq/Abdulrazaq, Abdulrasheed, Abdulrauf, Abdulsalam/Abdusalam/Abdusmall, Abdulwahab, Abduna, Abdurrahim, Abdurrashid, Abdusakum, Abdul/Abd, Abina, Abubajar/Abubakar/ Ababakar/Adubakari/Abu, Adam/ Adama/ Adamu/ Ado/Adu/Adang, Adhama, Adl, Afu, Ahmad/ Ahmadu/Ahmed,[23] Ajouma (born on Friday), Akilu, Akwala (king), Alarabe/Alarba (born on Wednesday), Alfa/Alifa (intimate), Alhali (liberator), Alhamadu, Alhamisu, Alhassan/ A-lasan/Al-Hassan, Ali, Alitaha, Aliu/Aliyu, Alkalawa, Alkali, Alkama (the upright), Alkassim, Almadu, Almustapha, Al-Otaiby, (the representative), Altine (born on Monday), Aluf (companion), Amadu, Amale/Amalu (worker), Aman, Amar/Ammar, Amin/Amina/Aminu, Ansari, Arzika (prosperity, sustenance), Arzula (belongs to God), Ashiru (companion), Askia, Ata, Atafi (the migrant), Attahir/Atahiru/ Atta (the virtuous), Auwalu /Awali (the first), Ayuba, Baba/Babah, Babandi/ Babangida/ Babagida (head of the family), Babatunde (father comes again), Baahari/Bahari, Balarabe/Balarebe (born on Wednesday), Balewa, Bashari/Bashiru/Bashar/Bashir, Basma, Bawa (slave of God), Buka/Bukar/Bukari/Boukary/Bukuru, Busari (intelligent), Dankasum, Dan Azumi, Dan Fulani, Dan Kura (person of Kura), Dan Mali, Dan Umma (member of the community) Dan-Mallam, Danhassan, Danjuma (born on Friday), Danladali (born on Sunday), Danladi (born on Sunday), Danlami (born on Thursday), Danlawan (the first), Dauda, DanAsabe (born on Saturday), DanLami (born on Thursday), Dogo (tall), Duna/Yabaka (dark skin), El-Hassan, Elmi (knowledge), El-Nafaty (supporter), El-Tayeb, El-Yakub/El-Yakubu, Enaum, Fada/ Faddy (influential, chief), Fadlallah (God's grace), Faike (itinerant trader), Fanya (knowledgeable), Farid/Fari (unique), Faroug/Farouk/Faruk/ Faru, Fawaz/Fewaz, Gada (successor), Gafar (forgiver), Gagara (extraordinary), Galib (victorious), Gambo (born after twins), Gana (learner), Gane (perceptive), Habbu/Habu (loved) Habeeb/Habibu/Habibal (beloved), Hadeja/Hadejia/Hadi (person from Hadejia), Haider, Halady/Khalady/ Hali/ Halidu, Halil/Halilu/Khalil, Hamed/Hamid/Hamidu, Hamisu/Hamizu, Hamoud, Hamza/Hanza, Hanga, Haruna/Haro, Hashim/Haushim, Hassan, Hayetudeen, Husaimi/Husaini/ Husein/ Hussain/ Hussaini/ Hussani/ Hussen, Ibrahim/Chigari/Shigari, Idris/Idirise/Idrus/Idi, Ila/Ilu/Iliasu/Iliayasu/Iliyasu/Ilyasy, Imam/Iman, Inusaa, Isa/Isah, Isamala (God's name), Ishalki/ Ishaku/Ishaaq/Is-hak, Isiakuu/Isiaka/Iya, Ismaila, Jaafar/ /Jafaru, Jada (good   fortune), Jafar/Jafaru/Jaffa/Jaffar,

Jamal/Jamara, Jamil/Jamilu, Jawad, Jazzar, Jelani, Jibrilu/Jibrin/Jibri/Jibbo/Jibo, Kabara/Kabiru/ Kabir/Kabila, Kadara (predestined), Kadir, Kamal, Kamaludeen, Kamilu, Kano, Karami/ Karimu/Kari, Kasim/Kassem/ Kassim/Kassum, Khaleel/Khalil, Khan-Malik (powerful king), Khatoun, Labaran (born during Ramadhan), Ladan (reward), Lamido, Lateeph/Lateef, Lawal (the first one), Lawan/Laawang (the first one), Leiko/Gambo (born after twins), Liman (religious leader), Magaji (mayor), Mahammoud/Mahmmoud/Mahmoud/Mahmound/Mahmud/ Mamudu/Mamuda, Mahdi, Mai (owner), Maikano (person from Kano), Maikanti (store owner), Maikarim (generous person), Mai-Lafia (strong), Mallam/malam/Malami (teacher), Mamman, Mamuni/Mamunu, Manga, Mansoor/Mansour/Mansur,[24]Mohamed/ Mohammadu/ Mohammed[25] Momuda, Muhtari/Mutari/Mukhtar/Muktar/Muktari/Mukthari, Murtala/ Muritala/Murta, Musa, Musdapher/Mustafa/Mustapha, Na-allah, Nagib, Najada,

Nalado/Dan Ladi (born on Sunday), Na-Nana, Nasaba (good lineage), Na-Sani (the second), Nasir/Nasiru, Nasirullai, Nasoro, Nassarawa/Nasarawa, Na-Zangi, Nazar/Nazara, Noureldin, Nufawa (benefit), Nuhu, Nura, Omar, Osiman/Osmoan/Osuman/Othman/ Ansamana, Qada, Qwaram (master), Rabah (gain) Rabiu/Rabi'u,

Radda, Rafin/Rafi (source of comfort),
Rahman/Rahaman, Raji, Ramzi, Rasheed, Rufai,
Saadu/Sedou/Saad, Saaibu, Sabaru, Sabiu, Sabo,
Sadigi/Sadik/Sadiq/Saduiki, Saeed/Said/Saidu,
Safiyanu, Saiyadi, Salahu, Salam/Salami,
Sale/Saleh/Salihi/Salihu, Salim,
Salisu/Sallsu/Sallisu/Salith (third), Salmanu/Salmon,
Saluhu, Samaila, Samalla, Samami/Sama/Sami,
Samusdeen, Sani/Sambo (second), Sanusi,
Sarki/Sarkin, Sauda, Sayodun/Sayudi, Sha'abu/
Shaaibu/Shaibu, Shafaatu, Shagari,
Sharif/Shariff/Sharrif/Sherif, Shehu/Sheehe/Shiekh,
Shiabu, Shinkafi/Shinku, Shittu, Shu'aibu/Shuaibu/
Shuaidu, Shuailu, Shukura, Sidi, Sifikin/ Sipikin/Sinkin,
Sinyudi/Siyudi, Soda, Sofiyanu, Suaudu, Sudawa,
Sulaiman/Suleiman/Suleman/Sule, Suleh, Sumaila,
Suwaid, Tafida/Tafidan/Tafdi, Taha, Tahir, Tarik, Tawil,
Tijani/Tijjani, Umar/Umaru/Umoru, Usama, Usanni,
Usmaini/Ansamana/Usman/Usmanu, Uyak, Wada
(wealthy), Wakeel, Wali/Waliyi, Wani (weak), Waru
(pious), Washe/Washoo (adorn), Waziri, Yaba/Yabo
(praised), Yaha/Yahya/Yahaya, Yakinni, Yakubu,
Yakudima (brave, vanguard), Yalwa/Yelwa, Yaminu,
Yanbani, Yanusa, Yari/Yauri (chief), Yassin, Ya'u, Yaya
(brother), Younes/Younis/ Yunusa, Yusif/Yusifu/
Yusuf/Yusufu, Zaharaddeen/Zahradden, Zain/Zeni/Zein,
Zakar/ Zakari/Zakariya/Zakoriya/Zaki/Zakirai,
Zawai/Zawiyya, Zia-Uddin, Zubairu.

HAUSA-FULANI FEMALE NAMES

Abarta (leave her to ward off evil eye), Adama (born on
Friday), Afere (tiny), Agwidu/Gwide/Gwisa (short),
Aisha/Aissata, Ajiji (on the rubbish to ward off evil),
Amina/Minata (trustworthy),
Asabe (born on Saturday), Atine/Altine/Tine (born on
Monday), Auta (youngest), Ayas (throw her away to

ward off evil), Baiwa/ Balwa/Bawa (slave, keeps away evil), Balaraba/Bala/Laraba (born on Wednesday), Baranka (blessings), Baturiya (born on Tuesday, wealthy girl), Bilkisu/Gado (the Queen of Sheba), Binti (daughter), Diza (nickname for Khadija/Hadija), Fadi (dim. of Fatsuma), Faji or Fati (dim. of Fatsuma, Fatimatan/Fatsuna/ Fenta/Fatsuna/Falmata, Firo (tiny), Gado (nickname for Bilqiis), Gaje (nickname for Fatsuma), Gajere (short), Gambo (born after twins), Giwa (elephant), Gudisa (short), Gujiba (short), Gwisa (short), Habiba, Hadija/Kedia/Khadija/Hadizatu, Halimatu/Halima, Hasaina, Hasana, Hawwa (born on Friday), Jimmo/Jummay (born on Friday), Kaka (born at harvest time), Kandala (lamp),Kandi (sweet), Kulu (born on Friday), Kumbula (short), Ladidi/Ladingo/ Ladi (born on Sunday), Lami/Laminde (born on Thursday), Leiko (born after twins), Magawata/Ganau (born on new moon), Maimuna, Mairama/Mairan Mairo/Maryam/Maryama, Narai (born on Wednesday), Nuru/Nura, Rabiatu (born on Wednesday), Ramata/Rama/Rahma, Roketou/Ruqaya, Salamatu/Salma, Saratu/ Sarai/Sara, Saudatu/ Sauda/Saude/Souwadou, Sharifiya, Shehara (famous), Talata (born on Tuesday), Tallafi/Talle (father or mother died soon after birth of the child), Tani/Tune (dim. of Atine), Turai/Bature/ Turawa (born on Tuesday), Uwa (mother), Yajja/Yarja (fair complexion), Yaya (elder sister), Yelwa (rich girl, prosperity), Zainabu/Djinabou/ Zeenaba/Abu, Zara/Zahra (flower).

Names such as Lasisi, Yakasai, Yamta, Yanbani, Larai and Mantai that are not easily identifiable as Islamic are left out from this list

SWAHILI MUSLIM MALE NAMES

Aamil	doer
Abadi	worshipper
Abas/Abasi/Abba [26]	stern
Abbakari/Abdakary	first Khalifa
Abdala/Abdalah/	
Abdalla [27]	God's servant
Abdallahman/	
Abdalrahman[28]	servant of the Compassion
Abde	servant
Abdel	servant
Abdi/Abdy/Abdu	servant
Abdilah/Abdilahi[29]	God's servant
Abdiqad[30]	servant of the Powerful
Abdow	servant
Abdubrahim	servant of Ibrahim
Abdul	servant
Abduldin	religious
Abdulaque[31]	servant of the Just
Abdulateef/Abdulatif	servant of the Gentle
Abdulaziz/Abdulazizi	servant of the Almighty
Abdulbahast[32]	servant of the Provider
Abdulbari/Abdulbary	servant of the Creator
Abdulbashir	servant of the Messenger
Abdulgawi	servant of the Strong
Abdulghafur/	
Abdulgafoor	servant of the Forgiver
Abdulghani/	
Abdulghany	servant of the Rich
Abdulgulam	servant of Ghulaam[33]
Abdulhakim	servant of the Wise
Abdulhamid	servant of the Praiseworthy
Abdulhalim	servant of the Gentle
Abdulhusein	servant of Husein
Abdulhussein	servant of Hussein
Abdulkader/Abdulkadir	servant of the Capable
Abdulkarim	servant of the Generous

Abdulkhalik/Abdulhalik	servant of the Creator
Abdulmajid	servant of the Exalted
Abdulmalik/	
Abdulmalek	servant of the King
Abdulnoor	servant of the Light
Abdulrahim	servant of the Compassionate
Abdulrasul	servant of the Messenger
Abdulrauf	servant of the Merciful
Abdulrazak	servant of the Provider
Abdulsattar/	
Abdulsatar	servant of the Protector
Abdulshakoor/	
Abdulshakur	servant of the Grateful
Abdulsultan	servant of the Ruler
Abdulswamad	servant of the Eternal
Abdultawabu	servant of the Forgiver
Abdultayar	servant of the Ready
Abdulwadud	servant of the Loving
Abdulwakil	servant of the Guardian
Abed/Abedi/	
Abeid/Abeda	young servant
Abeid	young servant
Abibu	beloved
Abid	devout
Abidali	servant of Ali
Abidhussein	servant of Hussein
Abu/Abuu	father
Abud/Aboud/Abood	servant/worshipper
Abuubakar	first Khalifa/Caliph
Adam/Adama/Adamu	Adam
Adamali	Adam+'Ali
Adamjee/Adamji	Adam+title of respect
Adan/Adinani	good fortune
Adhia/Adhiya	member
Adil	just
Afia/Afya/Afiah	health
Afidh[34]	protector

137

Afzal[35]	best
Aga	king
Aga Khan	noble king
Ahamad[36]	grateful
Ahluwalia	people+holy
Aiman	trustworthy
Aisha/Aysha	life
Akbar[37]	greatest
Akhtar/Aktar	star, chosen
Akiba	treasure
Akida	chief
Akile/Akil	intelligent
Akilimaji	wise+water
Akmal	most perfect
Akrabi	closest, intimate
Akubu	Jacob
Al-Abad	the permanent
Al-Abbas	the stern
Al-Adawi	the run
Aladin/Alladina	the religious
Alaiw/Alawi[38]	the great
Al-Alawy	the greatness
Alama	the sign
Al-Ameer	the prince
Alamin	the trustworthy
Al-Ammary	the lasting
Al-Amoody	the upright
Alarakhia	the happy
Alguhum	the bold
Alhabib	the beloved
Al-Haddad	the ironsmith
Alhaj/Al-haji/Alhaji	the pilgrimage
Al-Hamza	the drive
Alhasaniy	the good
Al-Hashr	the crowd, force
Ali/Alli[39]	exalted
Alireza	Ali+contented

Alishaan	Ali's character
Al-Jabry/Aljabri	the restorer
Al-Karim	the generous
Alley	prominent
Alma/Almas/Almasi	diamond
Al-Maawiy	the aquatic
Alnashir	the publisher, announcer
Alnasir	the protector
Al-Noor/Alnoor	the light
Aman/Amani	peace
Amana	trust
Amar/Ameir	prosperous
Ambari	ambergris
Amin/Ameen	trustworthy
Amin/Amini/Amyn	trustworthy
Amir[40]	prince
Amoda	dependable
Amor/Amour[41]	flourishing
Amrali	Ali's command
Amrani	cultured
Amri	bloom
Anar	bright
Anas	sociable
Anwar/Anwari[42]	brightest
Arif	knowledgeable
Arshad	wiser
Asgar[43]	youngest
Ashak	loving
Ashakali	loving+Ali
Ashakan/Ashok	loving
Ashoor/Ashour/Ashur	tenth of MuHarram
Ashraf	most honorable
Asif	intelligent
Aslam	safest
Asmatullah	God's protection
Assad/Assa/Assed	lion
Athman/Athuman/	

Athumani	third Khalifa
Atiya/Atiya	gift
Awadh/Awadhi	compensation
Awadhan	second compensation
Awale	first
Awan	helper
Awia	charmer
Ayam	the days
Ayoob/Ayub/Ayubu	Job
Azaad/Azad	greater
Azim	greatest
Aziz/Azizi	distinguished
Azmi	resolute
Azuni	powerful
Azuu	consolation
Azzan	most powerful

Baabeid	a person of the Abeids
Baakabe	a person of the 'Aqabs
Baalawy	a person of the 'Alawys
Baamar	a person of the 'Amars
Baamira	a person of the 'Amiras
Baasheith	a person of the Sheiths
Babu[44]	grandfather
Badar/Badr/Badru	full moon
Badi	outstanding
Badruddin	moon of the faith
Bagha	desire
Baghazal	a person of the Ghazals
Bahadur	the shining pearl
Bahamadi	a person of the Hamaadis
Bajaber	a person of the Jabers
Bajina	a person of distinction
Bakar/Bakari	short for Abubakar
Bakathiri	a person of the Kathirs
Bakhrani[45]	a person of the BaHrainis
Balahmar	a person of the AHmars
Bamusa	a person of the Musas
Baraka	blessing
Barkat	blessings
Baruti	gunpowder
Barwani	a tribe
Bashir	messenger
Bashueaib	a person of the Shu'aib
Baya/Bayani	evident
Benaya	edifice
Bilali/Bilal	the first Muadhdhin
Burhan/Burhani/	
Buruhani	proof
Burhanuddin	proof of faith
Busaidy	a person of the Sa'iids
Bushiri	joyful
Bwana	master

Dada	to pamper a child, sister
Dahir	fate
Dahoma	long life
Dahya	smart
Dakashi	twilight
Dalal/Dalali	middleman, broker
Daud/Daudi/	
Dauda/Dawood	David
Dawoodbhai	David+brother
Ebrahim/Ebrahimjee	Abraham+title
Esmail/Esmailijee	Ishmael+title of respect
Essa/Essajee	Jesus+title
Fadhel/Fadhil/Fadhili	outstanding
Faham	perceptive
Fahari	pride
Faheem	intelligent
Fahim	intelligent
Faisal	arbitrator
Faiz	victorious
Fakhili[46]	stallion, outstanding
Fakhruddin	pride of the faith
Faki	expert, legist
Fakihi	expert, legist
Fakir	poor, Sufi mendicant
Fakirmohamed	Faqiir+Muhammad
Farah	happiness
Farahan/Farahani	happiness
Faraj/Faraji	joy, relief
Fares	horseman, hero
Farhat	joy
Farid	unique
Farijala/Farijalah[47]	God's comfort
Farook/Farooq/	
Farouk	judicious, epithet for Khalifa 'Umar

Farooqui	judicious
Faswila	decisive
Fataki	fireworks
Fateh	victor
Fatehali/Fatehaly	victor+Ali
Fauz/Fauzi/Fauzy	successful
Fazal/Fazel/	
Fazil/Fezel	outstanding
Fazelabbas	Fazel+Abbas
Fedhela	excellence
Feisal	arbitrator
Feroz/Firoz/Feruzi	turquoise gemstone
Fida	redemption
Fidahusein/	
Fidahussein	Fida+Hussein
Firozali	Firoz+Ali
Fuad	heart
Fumbo	symbol
Fumbuka	bloom
Fundi	expert
Fundikira	learned
Fungo	success
Furaha	joy

Ghadhiyaka	well nurtured
Ghalib	victor
Gharib	visitor
Gharibe	visitor
Ghassant	to branch
Ghulam/Gulam	young, youth
Guhad	strive
Gulamali	young+Ali
Habeeb/Habib/Habibu	beloved
Habibullah	God's beloved
Hadi	divine ordinance
Hafeez/Hafidh/Hafidhi	preserver
Hafidh	preserver
Haidar/Haidari	strong
Haidarali/Haiderali	strong+Ali
Haider	strong
Hajee/Haji/Hajj	pilgrim
Haji/Hadji	pilgrim
Hajji/Hajo	pilgrim
Hakeem	wise
Hakim	wise
Hakimali	wise+Ali
Hakimjee/Hakimji	wise+title
Halas	stay, remain
Halfan/Halfani/Khalfan	successor
Hamad/Hamadi	gracious
Hamdan/Hamdani	praise
Hamdani	cool, soothe, calm down
Hamdoun/Hamdun	praise
Hamduali	praise+Ali
Hamduni/Hamdu	praise
Hamed	praiseworthy
Hameed	praiseworthy
Hamid	praiser
Hamidu	praising

144

Hamidy	praising
Hamil	dependable
Hamim	protector
Hamis/Hamisi	born on Thursday
Hammadi	praiser
Hammody	praiseworthy
Hamood/Hamoud/	praiseworthy
Hamoud	praiseworthy
Hamsini/Hamssin	fifty
Hamud/Hamudu/	
Hamuda	praiseworthy
Hamya	defender
Hamza	lion
Hamzaali	lion+Ali
Hamzia	Swahili classical poem

Hanafi	true believer
Hanga/Hange/Hango	reward
Hanif	true believer
Haq	justice
Harnani/Harunany	the second Aaron
Haroon/Haroun/	
Harun[48]	Aaron
Haroub/Harub	warrior
Harusi	wedding
Hasan	good
Hasanain/Hasnen	excellent
Hasanali	good+Ali

Hasania	merits
Hasham/Hashim/	
Hashimu	honor
Hashiim	honor
Hashil	emigrant
Hashmy	of the Hashimite
Hassain/Husein	good[49]
Hassam/Hassan	good
Hassan/Hosein	good
Hassanali	good+Ali
Hassanain/Hassnein	excellent
Hassani	good
Hassduna	they envied us
Hathian	hasten
Hatibu	orator
Hatim	resolute
Hatim/Hatimi	resolute
Hatimali	resolute+Ali
Hawa	Eve
Hazin[50]	judicious
Hebatullah	God's gift
Helem	gentle
Hemani	protected
Hemed/Hemedi	commendable
Heri	goodness
Hersi	guard
Hidayat	reward
Hifidh	protect
Hija	pilgrimage
Hilal/Hilali	crescent
Himid/Himidi	grateful
Hirji	out of difficulty
Hoja	proof, plea
Huseinal/Hussenail	good+Ali
Huseini	good
Husnain	good
Hussain/Hussein	good

Hyenin	they are alive
Ibrahim/Ibrahimu	Abraham
Idarous	young Idris
Idd/Iddi	festivity
Idrisa	Idris
Ikbal/Ikbai	good fortune
Ikhwat	brotherhood
Ilias/Iliyas/Ilyas	Elias
Imaan/Imani	faith, compassion
Imtiazali	assiduous
Imtiyaz	distinction
Inayat	bounty
InayatalIslam	bounty+Islam
Iqbal	good fortune
Isa/Isaa/Issa	Jesus
Isaac[51]	Isaac
Is-Hak/Ishaq	Isaac
Islam	Islam, safe
Ismael/Ismail/Ismaail	Ishmael
Issak	Isaac
Jaafar/Jafari[52]	small river, rivulet
Jabbi/Jaber	friendly, restorer
Jabey/Jabil/Jabir	courageous
Jaffar/Jaffer/Jafferr	rivulet
Jaffarali/Jafferali	Jaffer+Ali
Jafferaji/Jafferjee	Jaffer+jee
Jafferar /Jafferary	Jaffer+Ali
Jaha	prestige, esteem
Jahazi	well equipped, boat
Jalal/Jalala	majesty
Jama/Jamada/	
Jamadari	army general
Jamal	handsome
Jamalee/Jamali	beauty
Jamaluleyl	beauty+night

147

Jamil	goodlooking
Janabi	great
Janah	heaven
Jan Mohamed	Jan+Mohamed
Janmohamed	Jan+Mohamed
Januwalla/Janwalla	Jan+walla
Jaribu	attempt
Jarufu	cliff, strong
Jassam	great, immense
Jecha	sunrise
Jelan	great
Jemadari	army general
Johar/Johari	jewel
Juma/Jumah	born on Friday
Jumaa	born on Friday
Jumaan/Jumanne	born on Tuesday
Jumba	large building
Jumbe	chief
Kabiru/Kabiro[53]	great
Kabora	the best
Kadar[54]	destiny, able
Kademani	ancient ones
Kadernani	able
Kadibhai	judge+brother
Kadhey	judge
Kadhi	judge
Kaduma	old
Kaesa/Kaisi	firm
Kahatano/QaHTaan	legendary ancestor of the Arabs
Kahifan	cave man
Kaimu	leader
Kaindu	guide
Kaiyum	lasting, upright
Kalani/Karani	clerk
Kalenga	aim
Kale	ancient times

Kaluta	stern
Kamal/Kamala	perfection
Kamal/Kamali/Kamalia	perfection
Kamalkhan	perfect king
Kamaruddin/Kamrudin	full moon of the faith
Kambi	camp
Kanabi	messenger
Kanafani	protected
Kanani	explorer
Kaniz	treasurer
Karam/Karama	magnanimity, generosity, blessing
Karamali	magnanimity+Ali
Karata	playing cards
Karibu	welcome, near
Karim	generous
Karim/Karimi	generous
Karimbhai	generous+brother
Karimjee	generous+title
Karmali	magnanimity+Ali
Karume	master
Kasam/Kassam	just
Kasamala	God is just
Kasamali/Kassamali	just+Ali
Kasim/Kasimu/Kassim	just
Kassamah	elegance, justice
Kassamali	just+Ali
Kassamia	elegant
Kassanali	just+Ali
Kassim/Kassam	just
Kassima/Kassimu	just
Kassu/Kassum	just
Kazeni	companion
Kazi/Kazim	controller
Keis	rational, firm
Kermalli	kerm+Ali
Khaled/Kalid	lasting

Khalfa/Khalfan	successor
Khalid	lasting
Khalifa/Halifa/Khalif	successor
Khalil/Khalili	sincere friend
Khamasi	fifth
Khamis/Khamisi	born on Thursday, fifth
Khamsini	fifty, windy
Khan	ruler, title
Kharbush/Kharbusi	tent maker
Kharusy	a tribe
Khashimu[55]	respectful
Khassim[56]	
Khatib/Khatibu	orator
Khatrush	significant
Khatry	important
Khelef	successor
Kheri/Kherry	goodness
Kibwana	young master
Kilemba	turban, respect
Kindy	a tribe, soldier
Kisesa	story teller
Kombo	poor, defect
Konan	God wills
Kondo	warrior
Kubwa	great

Lila	good
Lodhi	seeks shelter
Lodhia	seeker of shelter
Lula	pearl
Lyellu	night
Maalim/Malim	teacher
Maamiry	a tribe, builder, firm
Maawy	a tribe, water carrier
Mabrouk[57]	blessed
Machano	born on Wednesday
Madadi	support
Madaraka	responsibility
Maftah	key to victory
Mahamdu	praised
Mahammed	praise
Mahdi	guide, leader
Mahfoudh/Mahfudh/	
Mahfudhi preserved	
Mahida	guide
Mahmood/Mahmoud	praised
Mahmud/Mahmudu/	
Mahmood[58]	praised
Maisara	ease
Majalio	destiny
Majaliwa	destined
Majid/Majidi	innovator
Majuto	regrets
Makame	ruler
Makata	poor, humble
Makini	serene, dignified
Malek/Malik[59]	king
Malekela	God is king
Malifedha	money is wealth
Malima	expert
Mamdali	Muhammad+Ali

Mamdani	Muhammad+Ali
Mandhry	a tribe, takes refuge
Manekia	immaculate
Maneno	words, orator
Manji	rescuer
Mansoor/Mansuri/	
Mansour	protected
Manssoor/Mansur	protected
Mansurali	protected+Ali
Maree	strength
Marjan/Marijani	red coral
Marjeby	a tribe, awed
Marzuk	blessed
Marzuku	blessed
Masauni	well protected
Mashaka	difficulty
Mashala/Masha	God's will
Mashkur	praiseworthy
Masika	heavy rains
Masikini	poor, humble
Masoud/Massud[60]	happy, fortunate
Massawe	equal rights
Matama	perfection
Matano/Machano	born on Wednesday
Matata	trouble
Maulana	our master
Maulidi/Maulid	birthday of Prophet MuHammad
Mawani	replenishment
Mayasa	pride
Mazhar/Mazher	manifestation
Mazrui/Mazruiy	a tribe, cultivators
Mbarak/Mbaraka[61]	blessed
Mbarakoot	blessed
Mbega/Mbegha	chief
Mbita	quiet
Mbogo	buffalo, spokesman
Mbwana	master

Mdoe	defendant
Mehar/Maahir	expert
Mehboob/Mehbub	beloved
Mehboob/Mahbub	beloved
Mehboobali/Mehbubali	beloved+Ali
Mehdi	guide, leader
Mehmuda	praised
Mfalme/Mfaume	king
Mganga	medicine man
Mgeni	guest
Mhamed/Mohamed[62]	praised
Mhina[63]	comfort
Mickidadi/Mikidadi	big and strong
Migila	productive
Miraji	Prophet MuHammad's ascension
Mirambo	well bred
Mkadamu	vanguard
Mkindi	a person of the Kindi tribe
Mkubwa	senior, great
Mmanga	emigrant from Oman
Mohamad	praised
Mohamed/Mohammed	praised
Mohamedali	MuHammad+'Ali
Mohamedally	MuHammad+'Ali

Mohamedaziz	MuHammad+Aziz
Mohamedbhai	MuHammed+Bhai
Mohamedhusein	MuHamed+Husein
Mohamedhussein	MuHamed+Hussein
Mohameditaki	MuHammed+Taqi
Mohamedkhan	MuHamed+Khan
Mohamedrafiq	MuHamed+Rafiq
Mohamedraza	MuHamed+Raza
Mohamedsadiq	MuHamed+Sadiq
Mohamedtaki	MuHamed+Taki
Mohammedabbas	MuHammed+Abbas
Mohammedali	MuHammed+Ali
Mohammedhussein	MuHammed+Hussein
Mohamood[64]	worthy of praise
Mohindeen/Muhidin	revivalist
Mohsen/Mohsin/	
Mohssein	beneficent
Mohsinali	beneficent+'Ali
Msafiri	traveller
Msallam/Mselem/	
Mselemu[65]	flawless
Msham/Mshamu	Syrian, hope
Mshamanga	hope+emigrant
Mshangama	avenger
Msoma	reader
Mstafa	chosen
Mtumai	hopeful
Mtumwa	messenger, servant
Mubarak	blessed
Mucadam/Mukadam	vanguard, leader
Mudrik	intelligent
Mugheiry	a tribe, bold
Muhajir/Muhaji	emigrant
Muhami	defender
Muhiddin/Muhidini/	
Muhidin	revivalist
Muhsin	beneficent

Mulla	religious
Mummin	believer
Mumtaz	excellent
Munif	exalted
Munim	benefactor
Munir	brilliant
Munir/Munira	brilliant
Munishi	close friend
Munisi/Munissy	close friend
Muqadam	vanguard
Murad/Muradi	good intention
Murji	hopeful
Murtaza/Murtaz	satisfied
Musa/Mussa	Moses
Musaji/Mussaji	Moses+title
Mushtaq	longing
Muslim/Muslimu	secure
Mussadiq	trustworthy
Mustaf/Mustafa	chosen
Muzaffer	victor
Mwalim/Mwalimu	teacher
Mwamba	strong rock
Mwanga	light
Mwinyi	ruler
Mwinyihatibu	Mwinyi+Khatibu
Mwinyihija	Mwinyi+Hija
Mwinyijuma	Mwinyi+Juma
Mwinyikambi	Mwinyi+Kambi
Mwinyikombo	Mwinyi+Kombo

Mwinyimkuu	Mwinyi+Mkuu
Mwita	caller
Mzaham	unique
Mzaina	adorns
Mzaituni	olive tree
Mzamil	companion
Mzee	elderly
Naaman	blessings
Nabhan	sensible
Nadeem	companion
Nadir/Nadur	rare
Naif	exalted
Naiman/Naimani	blessed
Naji	confidant
Najim	star
Najmi	starlike, astrologer
Najmuddin	star of the faith
Najmudean	star of the faith
Nanji	safe
Narmin	enlightened
Nasib/Nasibu	luck
Nasoro/Nasser/Nasso	saved
Nasrullah	saved by God
Nassar/Nasser/Nassir	triumphed
Nassery	triumph
Nassor/Nassoro/	
Nasoro	saved
Nathoo/Nathu	prominence
Naushad	aspired
Nazim	organizer
Nazir	foremost
Nazmudin	organizer of the faith
Ngome	fort, strength
Nizam	order
Nizar	keen eyed
Nizarali	Nizar+'Ali

156

Noor/Nur/Nuru	light
Noorali/Nurali	Noor+'Ali
Noorani/Noorany	light
Noorbhai	light+brother
Noordin/Nooruddin/	
Nurdin	light of the faith
Noorkarim	Noor+Karim
Noormohamed/	
Nurmohamed	Noor+Mohamed
Nyumba	house, fortified
Omari/Omar/Omary	the second Khalifa
Osman/Othman/	
Uthman[66]	the third Khalifa
Pandu	royal, artist
Pesa	money
Pili/Pilly	second
Qadir	capable
Qullatein	highest point
Quraishy/Quresh/	
Qureshi	a tribe
Qusai	firm
Rabii/Rabii'	spring, pleasant
Raffiq/Rafiki	companion
Rahim	compassionate
Rahimia	compassionate
Rahman/Rahmani	merciful
Rajab/Rajabu	7th month of Muslim calendar
Rajabali	Rajab+Ali
Ramadhan/	
Ramadhani/Ramazan	9th month of Muslim calendar month of fasting
Ramzanali	RamaDaan+'Ali
Rashad	sensible
Rasheed	intelligent

Rashid/Rashidi	intelligent
Rasool/Rasul	messenger
Raza/Razak/Razac	provider
Razahusein	RamaDaan+Hussain
Rehamtulla[67]	God's compassion
Rehan	sweet basil
Rehman/Rehmani	merciful
Rehmanji	merciful+title
Rehmudin	mercy of the faith
Riaz/Riyaz	sportsman, from riyaaD
Ridhwan	good will
Riyami	tribe of Riyam, resident
Riza	contented
Rizaz	contentment
Rizik/Riziki	blessings
Rizwan	good will
Rubama	possibility
Rubeya	nourishment, blessings

Saad/Saad/Saadi/ Saady	happiness
Saadun	happiness
Saakumi	four o'clock
Sabaah/Swabah	morning, pleasant
Sabbir	patient
Saber	patient
Sabit/Thabit	firm, reliable
Sabriye	patient
Saburi	patience
Sadak	told the truth
Sadalla/Sadallah	God's help
Sadar	appeared
Sadat	master
Sadik/Sadiki	friend
Sadikali	Sadik+'Ali
Sadiq/Sadique/Sadick	friend
Sadoun	good fortune
Sadridin/Sadruddin	vanguard of the faith
Sadru	vanguard
Sadrudin	vanguard of the faith
Saeed/Said/Saidi	happy
Safari	travel, journey
Sahib	companion
Saiffudin/Saifudin	sword of the religion
Saijad	worshiper
Saijadali/Sajjadally	Sajad+'Ali
Sajad	prostrate in worship
Sajam/Sajan	elegant
Sajjad/Sajjed	worshiper
Salaam	peace
Salah/Salahi	goodness
Salamy	peaceful
Saleem/Salim/Sallim	safe
Saleh/Salehe	good
Saleh/Swaleh/Swa	good
Salehmohamed	Saleh+Mohamed

Salimin/Salimini/Salmin/i saved
Salimu/Salum/Salumu safe
Sallah   goodness
Salman   safe
Samah   forgiveness
Samir/Sameer   entertainer
Samiullah   God's listener
Sattar   coverer, protector
Saudi/Saud   fortunate
Sayd/Sayed   master
Sefu/Seif/Seiff/Seifu sword
Seifdini/Seiffudin[68] sword of the faith
Senga/Sengo   bayonet
Senussi   Sufi order
Shaaban/Shaabani[69] 8th month of Islamic calendar
Shaban   8th month of Islamic calendar
Shabanali   Shaaban+'Ali
Shabbir[70]   religious
Shabib   youth
Shabirhusein   Shaabir+Husein
Shafi   healer
Shafiff   thin
Shafik/Shafiq   affectionate
Shah   king
Shahbudin   star of the faith
Shahdad   witness
Shaheed   witness
Shaheen   falcon
Shaib/Shaibu   elderly
Shakir/Shakur/Shakuri thankful
Shakooor   thankful
Shambi   leader
Shams   sun
Shamshu   sun, strong
Shamshudin/
Shamsudin   the sun of the religion
Shamte   gray haired, old

Sharif/Shariff/Sheriff[71]	honorable
Shariffali	Shariff+'Ali
Shaukat	desired
Shawwal	10th month of Muslim calendar
Sheha/Sheikh	leader
Shekhuna	our leader
Shekimweri	She+Kimweri
Shemakame[72]	She+Makame
Shempemba	She+Mpemba
Shikeli	tribe of Shikeli, builder
Shiraz	Shiraz
Shwaibu/Shuwayb/	
Shuwaybu	tribe of Shu'ayb, popularity
Sidi	master
Sidik/Sidiq	truthful
Simba	lion
Siraj	light
Skanda	tranquil
Slim	peace
Slum	peace
Sood/Sud/Sudi	luck
Soud	luck
Sued/Suedi	young master
Sufian/Sufiani	windy, ships
Suhail	canopus
Suleiman/Selemani[73]	Solomon
Suleimanjee	Suleman+title
Sulemanjee/Sulemanji	Suleman+title
Sultan/Sultani	ruler
Sultanali	Sultan+'Ali
Sultanally	Sultan+'Ally
Swabah	morning, pleasant
Tabu	difficulty
Taha/Twaha	man, opening of 20th Sura
Taher/Tahir	clean
Taherali	Taher+'Ali

Tajani/Tejani/Tijani	a Sufi saint
Tajdin	the crown of the faith
Tajmohamed	Taj+MuHammad
Taki	God-fearing
Talib/Twalib/Twalibu	seeker of knowledge
Tamim/Tamimu/Tamimi	perfect of character
Tariq	star, visitor
Tawakali	leaving oneself in God's hands
Tawfik/Tawfiq	divine guidance
Tayabali	Tayib+'Ali
Taymuur	defender
Teja/Tejan/Tejani	the crown of time
Thaani	second
Thabit	steadfast, firm
Thanaa'	praise
Tharwat	power
Thuweni	second
Twaibu	agreeable, good
Ubwa	delicate
Uki	impediment
Uledi	young man
Umar/Umari/Ummar	the second Khalifa, longevity
'Umraan	prosperity
Usaama	lion, brave
Usi	difficulty
Uthmaan	the third Khalifa
Valli	leader
Vuai	fisherman
Wahab	giver
Waheed/Wahid	unique
Wajid	much, many
Wajihi	distinguished
Wakili	trustee
Walid	newborn, productive

Walimohamed	wali+MuHammad
Walli/Walii	holy person
Wazir/Waziri	vizier, advisor, minister
Yaf'al	he acts
Yahaya/Yahya	John, he lives
YaHmad	he praises
Ya'iish	he lives
Yakiin/Yaqiin	definitive
Yakub/Yakubu[74]	Jacob, James, Akub
Yakubali	Yakub+'Ali
Yakuti/Yakout	sapphire
Yamani	from Yemen, blessings
Ya'mar	he lives long
Yasin	title of Sura, principle
Yassir	ease
Yaziid	he increases
Yousif	Joseph
Yunus/Yunusu	Jonah
Yusri	he makes it easy
Yussuf/Yusuf[75]	Joseph
Yussufali/Yusufali	Yusuf+'Ali

Zaakhir	generous
Zafer/Zaffer	successful
Zagar	restrain
Zaghluul	quick, industrious
Zahabu[76]	gold
Zahid	abstinent
Zahir/Zahiri	radiant, blossom
Zahor/Zahoro/Zahur	blooming
Zahran	shine
Zaidi	abundance
Zain/Zein	beauty
Zainuddin	Zain+diin
Zakaria/Zacharia	Zacharias
Zaki	guiltless
Zakir	remembrance
Zakirhussein	Zakir+Hussein
Zakiuddin	Zaki+diin
Zakwani	thriving
Zamani	long time ago
Zamiil	friend
Zarooq	dark complexion
Zawadi	gift
Zawawi	a tribe, the people of the Zaawiya
Zaydar	link
Zayduun	increase
Zhuher	shining
Ziada	addition, growth
Zidadu	abundance
Zidikheri	more blessings
Zubair/Zubeir/Zuberi	brave
Zuher	shining
Zulfikar	wise
Zulfikarali	wise+'Ali
Zume	manly
Zuri/Zuhri	goodlooking
Zuwein	goodlooking

SWAHILI MUSLIM FEMALE NAMES

Some of the names in this list are from the two East African directories mentioned earlier. Others are from my previous book, *What's In A Name*, from Swahili literary works, names given by friends and from personal knowledge of the region.

'Abla	wild rose
'Adhra	apology
'Adila/Adila	just
'Adla	justice
'Afaafa/Afafa	virtue
'Afifa/Afifa	virtuous, pure
'Afiya	health
'Afua	forgiveness
'Aida	gain, advantage
'Aisha/Eshe/Asha	alive
'Ajla	quick
Ajra	reward
'Alama	sign, symbol
'Aliya	exalted
Amali/Amal	hope
Amana	trust
Amiina/Amina	trustworthy
Aminabai	sister Amina
Amira/Amyra	princess
Amna/Amne	harmonious
Amra	powerful
Anisa/Aneesa	companion
'Arafa/'Arifa	knowledgeable
Asatira	legendary
Ashura	born on the first day of MuHarram
Asila/Asile	noble origin
Asiya/Aasiya	console, powerful
Asma	most exalted
Asmahaan/Asmahani	most exalted, ruler
Asumini/Yasmin	jasmine

165

'Atiya/Atiya	gift
'Aziza/'Azizeh/'Azzu	precious
Azmina/Azmina	determination
'Azza/Aza	powerful
Badra	moonlike
Badriyya	moonlike
Bahiyya	beautiful
Barke	blessings
Bashira/Bishara	predictor of good news
Basma	smile
Batuul	chaste
Bilqiis/Bilqees	Queen of Saba', Shibaa
Bushra	announcer of good news
Daaliya	black grapes
Daaniya	close, intimate
Daariya	informed
Dalila	proof
Dhakiyya	smart
Durra/Durrii	large pearl
Faaiza	victorious
Fadhila	outstanding, abundance
Fadya/Fadiya	redeemer
Fahima	learned
Faida	benefit
Faika/Faaiqa	superior
Fakharia	dignified
Fakhta/Faakhita	wild pigeon
Farashuu/Farshuu	butterfly
Fardaus/Firdaws	paradise
FariHa	joyful
Fariida	unique
FaSiiHa	eloquent
FatHiya	triumph
Fatmabai	sister

FatmaFatmah/Fatma"	Prophet MuHammad's daughter
FaTna/FaTina	intelligent
Fawziya/Fauzia	successful
Feroz/Ferozi/Firoz/e	turquoise
Firyaal	extraordinary
Fursiyya	heroism
Ghaaliba	successful
Ghafuura	forgiving
Ghaliya/Ghaalye	precious
Ghanima	great benefit
Ghaniya/Ghaaniya	rich, contented
Gharibuu	visitor, stranger
Ghaya	purposeful
Habiba	beloved
Hadia/Hadiya	gift
Hafidha/Hafidhuu	mindful
Hafsa	sound judgment
Haiba/Haibe	esteem
Hakima	sensible, wise
Hala	glorious
Halima/Haleema	gentle
Hamida	praises
Hanaa'	happiness

Hanifa	pure
Harbiyya/Harbuu	fighter
Hartha	productive
Hasanaat	merits
Hasina	beautiful
Hasnaa'	beauty
Hawa	Eve
Hayaat	life
Helemu	gentle
Hiba	gift
Huda	guidance
Hujayja	evidence
Husna	most beautiful
Ibtisaam	smile
'Iffat	virtue
Ilft/Ulfat	friendship
Ilham	inspiration
Imaan/Imani	faith
'Inaaya	providence
IntiSaar	victory
I'tidaal	upright
Jaha	prominence
Jahi	prominence
Jahiyya	prominent
Jamila/Jamilah	beautiful
Janat	heaven
Jasiira	courageous
Jawhara	gem
Jokha	embroidered brocade
Juwayriya	damask rose
Kaafiya	self sufficient
Kaamila	perfect
Kaasiba	gained
Kaatiba	writer

168

Kaatima	keeps secret
KaaZima	self control
Kamiila	perfect
Kamiliya	perfect, flower
Kariima	generous
Karma	generous
Kaukab	star
Kauthar	lady, river in heaven, star
Kesi	exemplar
Khadija/Katija/Hadija	Prophet MuHammad's first wife
Khamisa/Khamisuu/	
Hamisuu	fifth, born on Thursday
Khatoon	prominent
Khola/Khawla	deer, beautiful
Khuzaama	lavender
Khuzayfa	delicate as porcelain
Khuzayma	lavender
Kinaaz	fat
Kulthum/Kulsum	beautiful face
Laaiqa	worthy
Laami'a	glitters
Lam'a	flash of light
Lamii'a	glitters
Lamiis	soft
LaTiifa	gentle
Layla/Lela[78]	night
Liin/Liina	graceful
LiTaafa	gentleness
Looza	almond
Lubaaba	essence, heart
Lubayba	intelligent
Lubayya	young lioness
Lubna	resin, precious
Lulu	pearl
Lyutha	the wealth

169

Maahira	clever
Maajida/Majiida	honorable, glorious
Maariya	fair complexion
Ma'aSuuma	impeccable
Ma'atuuqa	emancipated
Mabruuka	blessed
Madaniyya	civilized
MadiiHa	praiseworthy
MaHbuba	beloved
Mahdiyya	guided
MaHfuuZa	protected
MaHmuuda	praiseworthy
Majda	honorable
Malaika	angel
MaliiHa	pleasant
Maliika/Malikia	queen
MarDiyya	satisfied
Marjaan/Marjani	red coral
Maryam/Mariyam[79]	Mary
Mas'ad	happy

Masarra	happiness
Maskiin/Maskini	humble, poor
MasmuuHa	forgiven
Mastuura	well covered, protected
MasTuura	fabulous, legendary
Mas'uuda	fortunate
Mathnaa	praise
Maulidi	birth of Prophet MuHammad
Mawduuda	loved
Mayaasa	walks proudly
Maymuuna	blessed
Maysaa'	walks with pride
Maysara	ease
Meyya	monkey
Meyya/Meyye	Mary
Meyyaan	dual of Meyya
Mina	fortunate
Moza/Moze/Mozza	distinguished
Muaddiba	well mannered
Mufiida	beneficial
Muhaymina	protector
Muhimma	important
Mujaahida	strive
Mu'mina	believer
Mumtaaz/Mumtaaza	distinguished
Muna	hope
Munira	brilliant
Muusira	rich, contented
Muzne/Muzna	rain clouds
Mwajabu	mwana+'ajaab=wonder
Mwaka	new year
Mwakheri	mwana+khayr=good
Mwanafatima	mwana+FaTma
Mwanahaji[80]	mwana+Hajj
Mwanahamisi/Mwanakhamis	mwana+Khamiis
Mwanahawa	mwana+Hawa
Mwanaidi	mwana+Idd

Mwanaisha	mwana+'aisha
Mwanaiwan	mwana+'iwaan=help
Mwanajuma/Mwajuma	mwana+Juma
Mwanakamba	mwana+kamba=rope
Mwanakatwe	mwana+qaT'=positive
Mwanakombo	mwana+kombo=difficulty
Mwatabu	mwana+tabu=difficulty
Mwatatu	mwana+tatu=three/Monday
Mwema	good
Naabiha	alert
NaaDira	beautiful
Nafaa/Naafiya	exiled
Naafi'a	beneficial
Naaila/Nayla	gain
Naajida	courageous
NaajiHa	successful
Naajila	generous
Naajya	saved
NaashiTa	active
NaaSifa	just
NaaSira	helps others
NaaZima	organizer, composer
Nabiila/Nabeela	noble, beautiful
Nadiima	companion
Nadra/Naadira	scarce
Nadya/Nadiya	magnanimous, generous
Nafiisa	priceless gem
Nafisa	comforter
Nafla	gift
Nahaar	daylight
NaHiifa	thin
Na'iima	comfort
NajaaH	success
Najma	star
Naqiyya	immaculate
Nargis	narcissus

NaSiiba	lucky
Nasiim	fresh breeze
NaSra/Nasrat/Nassra	help
Nawal	benefit
Nayfa	exalted
Nayfiin	benefited
Naysoun	dangling grapes, April, Spring
NaZiifa	clean
NaZiira	highest rank
Ne'ma/Neema	blessings
Ni'ma/Ni'mat	blessings
Nisreen/Nisriin	wild rose
Nunuu	extol

Nur/Nuru/Nurah	light, brightness
Noorjehan	noor+jehaan
NuSayba	young luck
NuSra	help
Nuzha	pleasure, fun

Qadiira	powerful
Qaadira	able
Qamariya/Qamar	like a moon
Qawiyya	strong
Qudsiyya	pious, holy
RaabiHa/Rabiha/	
RibaaH	gain
Raaghiba/Raghiba	desire
Raaiqa	beautiful
RaajiHa/Rajiha	victorious
Raajiya/Rajaa'	hopeful
Raamiya	star, marksman
Raatiba/Ratiiba	firm
Raawiya	story teller, entertainer
Rabii'a/Rabi/Rabia	spring, pleasant
Rabwa	well raised, growth
Radhiya/Raziya	contented
Rafii'a /Rafia	exalted, rising
Rafiida	benevolent
Rafiiqa/Rafika	companion
Rafiya	dignified
Raghiida/Raghda	good life
Rahiifa	dainty
RaHiila	strong
RaHma/Rahima/	
Rehema	compassion
Raiba	mature, perceptive
RaiHaana/ReHaana	sweet basil
Raiifa	gentle
Raiisa	leader
Ramla	divination
Ramza	symbol, sign
Ranaan/Raaniya	resonate
Raniima	beautiful voice
Rashida	wise, righteous
Rashiida/Raashida/	wise, righteous

174

Rashiiqa	charming
RaSiina	intelligent
RaTiiba	soft, gentle
RawHa	comfort
Raya/Rayah/Reyye	flag, vision
RayHa	small comfort
Rayyaan	luxuriant
Razina/Raziina	strong, patient
RiDwaana	contented
RiHaab	vastness, welcome
Riim/Reem	white gazelle
Riziq/Riziki	sustenance, luck
Rubeya	well bred, educated
Rukia/Rukiya/Rukiyah	superior
Rummaana	pomegranate
Ruqayya/Rukaya	superior
Ruzna/Ruzuna	well composed, calm
Sa'aada/Sada	happiness
Sa'adiyya	happy, lucky
Saa'ifa	helper
Saajiya	serene
Saarah/Sara	joyful, Prophet Ibraahiim's wife
SaaTi'a	radiates
SabiiHa/SabiHa	beautiful
Sabira/Sabra	patient, endurance
Sadiiqa/Sadika	trustworthy, friend
Safiyya/Safia/Safiya	immaculate
Sa'iida/Saida/Saide	happy
Sajeda/Saajida	worshiper
Sakhiyya	generous
Sakina/Sukaina	calm
Salama/Salma[81]	peace
Salha	considerate
Salwa	solace
Samha	magnanimous
Samia/Samii'a	listener
SamiiHa/Samiha	forgiving

Samiira/Samira	companion, entertainer
Saniyya	majesty
Sanura	kitten
Sariyya	noble
Sauda	black lady, Prophet MuHammad's wife
Saumu	fasting
Sayyida	lady
Sebtuu	born on Saturday
Shaadiya	praise, commend
Shaafi'a	mediator
Shafii'a	mediator
Shafiiqa/Shafika	kind
Shafuuqa	
Shahiira	famous
Shahrazad	princess
Shaida/Shayda	celebrate
Shaima	astute
Shakiila	well formed
Shamim	sweet scent
Shamsa/Shemsa	sunlight
Shani	significant
Shariifa/Sharifa[82]	honorable
Shawana	grace
Sheikha/Shekha	leader
Shufaa/Shifaa	healing
Shukuru	be grateful
Shuruuq	dawn
Siddika/Sidika/Siddiiqa	honest
SiHaaba	philanthropist
Siham	participation
Siti/Sitti	lady
Siwaara	bracelet, ornament
Su'aad	happy
Subira/Subra	patience
Suhaila	ease
Sulayma	safe

SulTaana	ruler
Sumayya	good reputation, high rank
Sumra/Sumira	brown
Surayya	noble
Surura	happiness
Suusaan	beautiful plant
Su'uuda	happiness
Suwayda	black

Taahira/Tahira	neat
Taanisa	sociable
Tabassam/Tabasamu	smile
Tafiida	benefit
TaHiyya/Tahiya	security
TalHa	easy life
Taliba	seeker of knowledge
Tama'a/Tamaa	ambition
Tamia	impeccable
Taqiyya	God fearing
Tashrifa	honoring
Tasniim	elevate
Tathmiina/Tathmina	precious

Tatu	three, born on Monday
Tausi	peacock
Tawfiiqa	success
TawHiida	believes in one God
Tawiilu/Tawilu	tall
Tayba/Tayyiba	pleasant
Taymuura	guardian
Thureya/Thurayya	Pleiades
Thuwayba	small gift
Tifla/Tefle	infant
Titi	dark
TuffaaHa/Tufaha	apple
TuHfa/Tuhfa	gift
'Ubaada	worshipper
Ubah	flower
Umayma	young mother
UmKulthuum	Prophet MuHammad's daughter
Ummi/Umi	my mother
Umsa'ad	happy mother, Sa'ad's mother
Waabila	heavy rains
Waafiya	loyal
Waathiqa	hopeful
Wadaa'a	gentleness
Wadi'a/Wadii'a	established
Wafaa	accomplishment
Wafiiqa	agreeable
Wahba	philanthropist
Wahiba/Waahiba	gift
WaHida	unique
Wajiiha	distinguished
Waliyya	ruler
Warda	rose
Wardiya	rosy
WaSiifa	praiseworthy
WaTiyya	cooperator

178

Wifaaqa	harmony
Yafi'a	high rank
Yamiina	from Yemen
Yaqiina	positive
Ya'quuta	sapphire
Yasmin/Yasmina	jasmine
Yathriba	old name for Medina
Yumna	blessed, good luck
Yusra	ease and comfort
Yusriya	makes things easy
Yuuthar	plentiful
Zaafarani	saffron
Zaahida	satisfied
Zaahira	radiate
Zaakhira	generous
Zabibu	grapes
Zahara/Zahra	flower, beauty
Zahiya	beautiful
Zaina	beautiful, elegant
Zainab/Zainabu/ Zaynab[83]	Prophet MuHammad's daughter and the name of one of his wives
Zaitun/Zaituni/Zeitun	olive, guava
Zaituuna	olive
Zakiya/Zakia	pure, excellent
Zaliikha	ahead, brilliant
Zamzam	holy water in Mecca
Zanbaqa	iris, beauty
Zariifa	graceful
Zarina/Zari	golden thread
Zawadi	gift
Zayana/Zeyana/ Ziyana	elegance
Zehra /Zera	beauty
Zeina/Zena/Zennah/	

Zaina	adornment
Zeyana	adornment
Zinah/Zina	ornament
Zubeda/Zubeida	best
Zuha	attractive
Zuhayra/Zohra/Zuhera	beautiful
Zuhra/Zuhura	beauty, Venus
Zulekha/Zuleikha/	ahead, brilliant
Zulfa/Zulfat/Zalfaa	likes to please
Zumarrad	emerald
Zuweina/Zuwena/	
Zuena (dim. of Zena)	beautiful

Abbreviations

dim.	diminutive	'	Arabic
f.	feminine	'	Arabic
m.	masculine	D/d̲	Arabic
sg.	singular	H/h̲	Arabic
pl.	plural	S/s̲	Arabic
d.	dual	T/t̲	Arabic
/	alternate form	Z/z̲	Arabic

NOTES

1. See his article on "African Proverbial Names" in Names Vol. 28 1980 p. 196.
2. Ref. Zawawi, 1993.
3. At first it is useful to include Nyang's concept of the African traditional man. See p. 20.
4. Sometimes a person in the Hausa-Fulani community may be known by his profession or occupation instead of his father's name.
5. The name appears with two spellings, Fadio and Fodio.
6. An Arabic equivalent with exactly the same meaning is mal `belonging to' but this is not used in naming in this way. Rather, a lexical item banuun or its abbreviated variant banuu or ba is instead and is attached to tribal names as in Banuu Haashim or Baalawi.

7. The chronological name for the first child has the following variations:auwal, lawal, lawali, lawan, and auwalu. The Romans used numbers such as Quintus (fifth), Octavius (eighth) and Septimus (seventh) as personal names.

8. The Swahili equivalent for the number five is tano and the name is Machano, but Hamisi or Khamisi is the name equivalent for a child born on Thursday.

9. The custom of naming a child by his or her day of birth is also common among non-Muslim Africans. See Zawawi ibid. p. 78 and on their use by African-Americans and others in the diaspora see J.L.Dillard's, Black Names.

10. See previous discussion on p. 118.

11. The source for these names is a Nigerian telephone directory.

12. See page 114 on NAMES AND THEIR SPELLING.

13. Sometimes all the three nonemphatic sounds Daad, Zaal and Dhaal are represented by one sound dh as in Fadhil for FaaDil and Haafidh for HaafiZ and Dhiyaab for Dhiyaab. The sounds zaal and dhaal are written as z as in Muzill for Mudhdhil and Aziz for `Aziiz.

14. As in Cheikh Anta Diop's name.

15. Two entries of Dauda and one of Daudi also appeared.

16. See pevious discussion on pages 96-103.

17. Although there is no feminine of the name Adam in Arabic it exists in Hausa-Fulani as Adama.

18. Since little research has been carried out on the subject of African Muslim names four telephone directories were used as primary sources for this study. These were the Nation Telephone Directory of Kenya (1992); the Tanzania Telephone Directory (1991-2); Nigeria Telecommunication Limited (1990); and Directory No. 276 of Permanent Missions to the United Nations (July 1995).

19. See p.161 for other variations.

20. See p.161 for more variations of the name.

21. See p. 166 for other spellings of the name.

22. Blyden, p. 278.

23. It also appears as Ahamed, Ahmadu and Amadou.

24. The name is also spelt as Mansuri and Mansury.

25. Numerous other spellings occur which include Moh'd, Mohd, Mommed, Mudi, Mame, Muhammadu, Muhammed, Muhammud, Muhamudu, Muhd and Mahammadu.

26. This name appears also as Abass, Abasy, Abbas, Abbasi and Abbass.
27. This name is widely used in both Kenya and Tanzania. It is also spelt as Abdullah, Abdallah, Abdala and Abdula.
28. It is also spelt as Abdulrahman, Abdurrahman, Abdarahman and Abdalahman.
29. Also Abdillah and Abdillahi.
30. This is an abbreviation of the name Abdilqaadir.
31. This may be an abbreviation of AbdulHaq the servant of the Just One.
32. Two entries appear. These convey a misspelling of the name AbdulbaaSit.
33. The youth referred to here is probably Imam Hussein.
34. The first letter H is dropped from HaafiZ.
35. This name is derived from AfDal 'better or best.' Here the sound z is substituted for the emphatic Z.
36. This name also appears as Ahamadi/Ahamed/Ahamedi/Ahmad/Ahmada/Ahmadi/Ahmed/Ahmedali/Ahmedi.
37. This name appears in this spelling and as Akbarali/Akbaraly/Akber/Akberal/Akberali and Akberhussein.
38. Also Alawy, Alwi, Allawy.
39. Also appears as Aly and Ally.
40. The name appears also in Tanzania as Amiral/Amirali/Amirally/Amiri/Amirudin and Amrudin.
41. Also Amur, Aamur and Amury.
42. Also appears in Tanzania as Anwarali and Anwary.
43. Appear in Tanzania also as Asger/Asgerali/Asgher and in Kenya as Asgar and Asghar.
44. The word in Kiswahili means grandfather and is also used by non-Muslims with names such as Jackson, Joshua and Maurice.
45. This might be a misspelling for BaHraani of BaHrein Islands in the Middle East.
46. This is a misspelling of faaHil stallion or bull.
47. Also Farijalla and Farjala.
48. This name appears also as Haruna and Haruni in Tanzania and in Nigeria.
49. This change of -n to -m is also seen in the name Waziin 'of sound judgment' which sometimes is spelt Waziim meaning in Swahili 'crazy,' not the intended meaning! Other examples are the changes from Roshan to Rosham and Sajan to Sajam.

50. This is an example of a change of m to n, instead of n to m. The other one is Kassam becoming Kassan in Kassanali.
51. Isaac is Is-haaq in its Muslim equivalent and in Tanzania appears with names such as Abeid, Juma, Suleiman, Abraham and Musa.
52. This name also appears as Jafer, Jaffar and Jaffari.
53. Appears also as Kabiri, Kabura and Kaburu.
54. The name appears in Tanzania also as Kadiri, Kadri, Kaduri, Kaduli and Kadu and in Kenya as Kadria, Kader, Kadiri, Kadir and Kadri.
55. This may be a misspelling of Haashim 'repectful' or Haashim a 'tribe.'
56. This is probably a misspelling of Qaasim /Kaasim 'just' rather than this form which means an opponent.
57. It appears also as Mabruck, Mabruk and Mabruki.
58. This name is also spelt in Tanzania as Mahmoud and Mahomoud.
59. Also Malick, Maliki and Malaki.
60. Also Massudy, Masud and Masudi.
61. It also appears in Kenya as Mubarak and Mbaruku and in Tanzania as Mbarouk, Mbaruck, Mbaruk and Mbaruku.
62. There are also examples of Mhamadi, Mohamedi, Mohammad, Mohammed, Mo'd, Moh'd, Mohamedy, Muhamed, Muhammad and Muhammed.
63. This name is used by Muslims and non-Muslims and appears with names such as Amani, Sultan, Joseph and John.
64. Also Mohamoud, Mohamud and Mohmood.
65. There are also Mselema, Mselem, Msellem, Msellemu, Musalam and Muselem.
66. Also Othmani, Othuman and Usman.
67. Other spellings that appear in Tanzania are Rehmtulla, Remtulla and Rhemtulla.
68. Also Seifuddin and Seifudin.
69. Also Shaban and Shabani.
70. In Tanzania we also get Shabbar, Shabbier, Shabir and Shabiro.
71. There is also Shariffu.
72. Many other names appear in Tanzania with the prefix she-.
73. The different spellings of this name in Tanzania include: Suleman, Sulaiman, Sulayman, Suleimani, Suleimana, Suleimain, Suleman, Sulemani, Suleyman, Seleiman and Seleman.

74. Also Yakobo and Yakoub.
75. Also Yussuph, Yusufu and Yusuph.
76. This is a misspelling of dhahab, gold.
77. This name also appears as Fatima, Fatuma, Fatima, Fatu, Fatumabai and Fatmabhai.
78. It also appears as Lailat, Lailah, Leila and Leluu.
79. Also Mariam, Mariamu and Mariambhai.
80. Mwana is a Swahili word for a woman.
81. Listed also Suluma, Salamuu, Salme, Salima and Sulayma.
82. This name also appears as Shareefa, Shariffa, Shareefe and Sharife.
83. It also appears as Zeinab, Zeynab, Zenab and Zainoo.

REFERENCES

Adamu, Mahdi, 1978, *The Hausa Factor in West African History*, Oxford University Press, London.

Al-Arnaa'uuT, Shafiiq, 1988, *Qaamuus Al-asmaa' Al-'ar biyyah*, Beirut.

Asante, Molefi Kete, 1991, *The Book of African Names*,Africa WorldPress, Inc. Trenton, New Jersey.

Blyden, Edward W., 1887, *Christianity, Islam and the Negro Race*, Edinburgh University Press, Aldine Publishing Company, 1967, Chicago.

Damali, Nia, 1986, *Golden Names for an African People*, Blackwood Press, Atlanta, Georgia.

Diop, Cheikh Anta,1974, *The African Origin of Civilization: Myth or Reality*, Lawrence Hill Books, Chicago, Illinois.

Doi, Ibrahim, 1969, 'Thought and Culture in Africa with Special Reference to Nigeria' in *The Islamic Review and Arab Affairs*, Vol. 57, pp.18-23.

Hathurani, Moulana Ahmad Muhammad, n.d.,*Names for Muslim Children*, Dawa Book Shop, California.

Mazrui, Ali A., 1986, *The Africans: A Triple Heritage*, Little, Brown & Company, Boston/Toronto.

Mazrui A. & I. Shariff, 1993, *The Swahili: Idiom and Identity of an African People*, Africa World Press, Trenton, New Jersey.

Nyang, Sulayman S.,1990, *Islam, Christianity and African Identity*, Amana Books, Brattleboro, Vermont.

Ojoade, J. Olowo,'African Proverbial Names:101 Ilaje
    Examples' in *Names, Journal of the American Society*,
    Vol. 28, No.2, June 1980.
Robert, Shaaban,1968, *Diwani ya Shaaban 6:Kielezo chaFasihi*,
    Nelsons & Sons, Tanzania.
Zawawi, Sharifa M., 1993, *What's In a Name? Unaitwaje?*,
    Africa World Press, Inc., Trenton, New Jersey.